the hole of the pit
are digged" (Isa. 51:1).

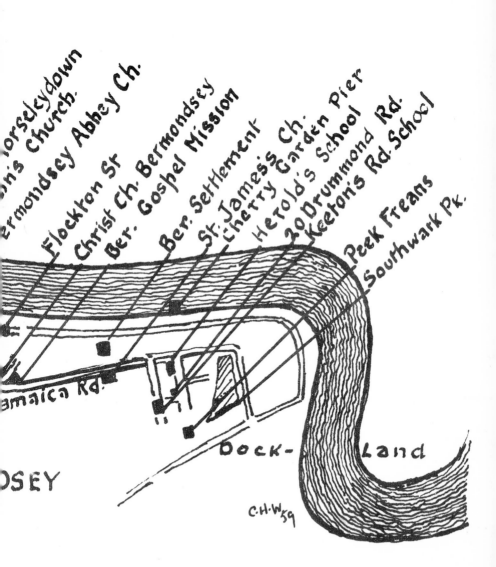

Horsleydown
...n's Church.
...ermondsey Abbey Ch.
Flockton St
Christ Ch. Bermondsey
Ber. Gospel Mission
Ber. Settlement
St. James's Ch.
Cherry Garden Pier
Herold's School
20 Drummond Rd.
Keeton's Rd. School
Peek Freans
Southwark Pk.

amaica Rd.

Dock-Land

...OSEY

C.H.W. 59

CHARLES H. WELCH

AN AUTOBIOGRAPHY

Principal of
The Chapel of the Opened Book
Wilson Street, Finsbury Square, E. C. 2.

Author of
DISPENSATIONAL TRUTH
LIFE THROUGH HIS NAME
JUST AND THE JUSTIFIER
and other works

For over 50 years
Editor of the *BEREAN EXPOSITOR*

Author of
an extensive Library of Tape Records
of expository addresses on the Bible.

1960

THE BEREAN PUBLISHING TRUST
40, Tumblewood Road, Banstead, Surrey,
England.

PREFACE.

When I was asked to write the Preface to my father's book I thought at first that the more intimate family viewpoint that I must inevitably have would be focussed on too many small and homely details, which could have no bearing on a book of this scope, and no value to future readers. As I read for myself however I realized that the family background, far from detracting from the main theme seemed to spotlight the essentials and provide the key to the whole book.

As a child I was of course unaware of the background of struggle and frustration that must have continually occupied my parents' minds. I became conscious that my father was engaged in something vaguely referred to as "The Work". It was obviously no nine-till-five job, forgotten in hours of relaxation - it was something that spilled over into every nook and cranny of our home. Startled plumbers or postmen, window cleaners or schoolfriends would suddenly meet an unconventionally garbed figure, and find themselves deep in a conversation concerning the meaning of a Greek word, or the unwary would hear the words "As Paul says ......", and learn more about the structure of an epistle in five minutes than they had ever known in a lifetime.

He was, and is, a man of many enthusiasms, individualistic, widely read and with wide interests, disconcertingly ready to joke, to deflate the pompous, to pull the leg of the stiff and starchy - yet all these complex sides to his character are ready to be subordinated to the one aim of his life - to preach the "unsearchable riches of Christ". His is no Sunday religion, but a way of living that absorbs the whole man.

The book you are about to read looks back to the humble beginnings in Bermondsey, and traces the way, step by step through the years. The struggles are there, the many closed doors, the humour and the heartaches; but looking back with him we can see how thorough was God's preparation for the task He had in mind, how unexpected, but how certain.

For as long as I can remember there has hung on the wall of my father's home a text from Philippians 3. It hangs here now in Beckenham, and at this time of his eightieth birthday, when he has spent much time in looking back and gathering together his memories of past years, it seems to me that it would be appropriate as a reminder that this is a most forward-looking book.

"This one thing I do, forgetting those things which are behind, and reaching forth unto those things which are before, I press toward the mark for the prize of the high calling of God in Christ Jesus".

Ruth Baker
Beckenham.
April. 1960.

Charles H. Welch.

ILLUSTRATIONS - The WHAT? and the WHY?

Suggesting the way in which the Potter uses environment, custom and upbringing, in the fashioning of His earthen vessels.

* * * * * * * *

THE END, in two meanings of the word; for here the story of the earthen vessel merges with the treasure that alone justifies this preamble and otherwise common-place piece of human conduct and history of a "Bermondsey Boy".

TREASURE IN EARTHEN VESSELS

The words at the heading of this opening section of an auto-biography are found in 2 Corinthians 4:7; the "Treasure" of the immediate context being "the glorious Gospel of Christ, Who is the image of God" (2 Cor. 4:4). Paul uses the word "ourselves" twice in the succeeding verse:-

(1) "We preach not ourselves, but Christ Jesus, the Lord; and

(2) "Ourselves your servants for Jesus' sake".

No one acquainted with the context of that "glorious gospel" could ever imagine Paul preaching about himself, yet it would not be stating fact if we ignored the many passages in his writings that emphasize the importance he attached to the ministry he had received, even though true humility compelled him to liken himself to an "earthen vessel". The epistle to the Galatians while ostensibly a defence of the basic doctrine of Justification by Faith, nevertheless devotes the whole of chapter one and a good part of chapter two, not to the "treasure" but to the "earthen vessel" that contained it, and this will be seen most clearly if the literary structure of chapter one be exhibited.

Galatians 1:1-24

A 1:1-5 Not, Neither, But. Paul's independent Apostle-
ship

A 1:11-12
Not, Neither, But. Paul's independent Gospel.

A 1:15-17
Not, Neither, But. Paul's independent Commission.

This structure is not complete, but as it is not our present purpose to give an exposition of Galatians, the above simple outline will be sufficient to demonstrate our contention, namely, that there is a divinely sanctioned relationship between:

"The Lord's message" and "The Lord's messenger" (Hag. 1:13).

Paul, among other things, is set forth as a "pattern" (1 Tim. 1:15, 16) and his teaching as a "form" (2 Tim. 1:13, where both "pattern" and "form" translate the same Greek word, *hupotuposis* ("a rough sketch, before the finished design"). It would be immodest and untrue to say that the subject of this Biography set out to model each step of his pathway on the lines of this great pattern, but a retrospect that looks back over more than half a century cannot help but recognize in many of the steps taken, of doors opened or shut, of timely interventions, and of gruelling disappointments, that some approximation, however sketchy, of the grand pattern given by inspiration of God has been unconsciously reached.

This autobiography deals more with the sovereign choice of the great Potter, and the disposal of all the shaping circumstances of time and place, heredity and environment, than with the glorious truth entrusted to it - the earthen vessel rather than the treasure in it.

The outpouring of this "treasure" has been the central feature of our ministry for the last fifty years, and the reader is asked to acquaint himself with the *Berean Expositor*, the *Alphabetical Analysis*, and the list of publications found on the back pages.

In this autobiography we are dealing mostly with common clay. Among the circumstances that were used in fashioning this unpromising material, were the influences of home, parents and school.

Over against these must be set the disadvantages of being born in Bermondsey - a district that could easily prompt the quotation:

"Can any good thing come out of Nazareth?"

The ideals of my parents, the attractions of both music and art, the devoted lives of one or two whose names are recorded and their influence recognized later in these pages all combined, under God, to shape and fashion the plastic clay of adolescence into the vessel foreknown by sovereign Love.

Following my conversion came four or five years of rigourous discipline wherein I must confess "I lived a Pharisee". This period proved to be the crucible used in finishing the earthen vessel. The fires were stoked with high Calvinism, Pharisaic Puritanism, a false application of the words "Touch not, taste not, handle not" and the effects on mind and character that "eternal conscious torment" even upon "unevangelized heathen" and "babes in slums" must most surely have.

Elsewhere we have given full credit to the positive teaching that this period provided, but the "perfecting work" was a discipline endured with much heart searching, questioning and bewilderment.

The final touch was the meeting with Dr Bullinger at Bury Street in 1908, when the "earthen vessel" which had been twenty eight years preparing was at last entrusted with the "Treasure" that alone makes this record of any worth.

We make no claims either to scholarship, or to superior sanctity, and writing this memorial so late in life, the feeling of awe and wonder still persists and finds an echo in the words of a greater and more consecrated servant:

"Unto me, less than the least of all saints is this grace given".

Whatever else the reader of the following lines may feel, he will at least find a semblance of such a passage as 1 Corinthians 1:27, 28.

"God hath chosen the foolish ... the weak ... the base ... yea the things that are not ... that no flesh should glory in His presence".

At the time of writing this Biography, the subject,   Charles H. Welch, has just reached his Jubilee as Editor of the *Berean Expositor*   and has about fifty books and booklets to his credit, all devoted to the exposition of the Scriptures, and all honouring that first principle of sound interpretation, namely "Right Division"(2 Tim. 2:15). No other periodical has stood squarely for the concept that Acts twenty eight and not Acts two constitutes the Dispensational Frontier, and no other publications set forth *the logical consequences* that follow the recognition of this Frontier, namely the unique ministry of Paul as the "Prisoner" of the Lord for us Gentiles, who alone, at the beginning, received the dispensation of the Mystery, hitherto "hid in God" (Eph. 3:1-13). Perhaps the unique character of this ministry will justify the following attempt to cover the early years of this very earthen vessel in the hope that others, intimidated by a similar humbleness of origin, and lack of academic qualifications together with the absence of any social advantages, may take courage from the example set forth in the following pages, and believe that "God's commands are also God's enablings".

Before embarking upon such a ministry that stood alone against Ritualist, Rutualist and Rationalist, that questioned the very foundations even of much that passes for Evangelical teaching, and which challenged "Churchianity" at its centre, it might have been expected that the vessel chosen would have had a College training and had some social standing; but the fact remains that he had neither a Christian upbringing nor any advantages, so-called, whatever, and could read with much sympathy the slur cast upon the Saviour in such words as "How knoweth this man letters, having never learned?"

"Hath not the Potter power over the clay, of the same lump to make one vessel unto honour, and another unto dishonour" (or unto a menial purpose)? (Rom. 9:21).

NO MEAN CITY

The genuine Londoner, even though born south of the Thames, claims an association with Bow Church, Cheapside, for any one born within the sound of Bow Bells is a cockney, a typical Londoner.

Mary-le-Bow

It is interesting to note that the city of London was first inwalled by Helen, the mother of Constantine the Great, about A. D. 306. This work was later raised and strengthened, and a wall eight feet thick and twelve feet in height was built.

London was earlier named Londium, Longidinum, and Lundinum. The Briton called it Lundayne; the Saxon Lundenceaster, Lundenbrig, and Londennir, but the inhabitants themselves called it just plain London, and so it is called to this day. Cheapside was originally called Westcheap, a name echoed in the vicinity of London Bridge by Eastcheap. The word "cheap" indicates a market, it is found in the names of English towns compounded with the word "Chipping", and is seen in the Danish equivalent Copenhagen. Branching off from Cheapside, streets still retain their distinctive market associations, as Bread Street, Milk Street, Wood Street and Poultry.

It may be of interest to record the localities that were used by various trades in early times.

Goldsmiths, the south side of West Cheape.
Drapers, first in Lombard Street, then Candlewick Street.
Skinners in Bridge Street and Walbrook.

Stock fishmongers in Thames Street.
Wet fishmongers in Knightrider Street and Bridge Street.
Ironmongers in Ironmonger Lane to Thames Street.
Butchers in Eastcheape.
Hosiers in Hosiers Lane and Cordwayners Street.
Shoemakers in Cordwayners Street and St. Martins Le Grand
and London Wall near Moorgate etc. , etc.

"It appeareth by records, that in the year 1302, which was
the 30th of Edward 1, the bakers of London were bound to
sell no bread in their shops or houses, but in the market"
(Stow).

Fryday Street (now Friday Street), which was parallel with
Broad Street, was so called by reason of the fishmongers
there, and the serving of fish in Friday's market.

Sidney R. Jones, in his book "London Triumphant" enthuses
over the church of St, Mary-le-Bow:

"Just look how the sun catches it, I said to Anthony as we
saw Bow Church rising serene over the rattle and traffic of
Cheapside. See how the old boy (i. e. Christopher Wren)
jumped off the square of the tower to the circular base of
the steeple, engaged the four tower corners with finials to
send the lines upward, and in delicate, lessening proportions
swept right up to the vane of the tapering spire".

This church was one of fifty-two city churches built or restored by Christopher Wren after the great fire of London.
In 1904 Sir Charles Stanford revived the old time chimes
"Turn again Whittington" thrice Lord Mayor of London. We
dare not allow our interest to cause us to loiter here however,
for our geographical centre lies across the river to the South
East. The reader's attention is drawn to the map that forms
an end paper of this book, to which reference will have to be
made as this pilgrimage proceeds. We therefore make our
way past the Mansion House and the Bank of England, affection-
ately called by the Londoner, "The little old lady of Thread-
needle Street". Stow speaks in 1598 of "Three Needle Street"
from the sign of the "Three Needles", but the origin of the
sign is a matter of conjecture and need not detain us.

The visitor to London should not omit a walk through Lombard Street, where many of those ancient coloured signs have
been revived. We proceed down King William Street, so named
after a statue of "the sailor King" which stood at the foot of
London Bridge, and cross the river to the South side. On our
left just as we reach the river side stood Adelaide House,
which was demolished in 1920, bringing to light one of the
arches of old London Bridge. A Roman bridge, the first to

cross the river cannot be described, but some reference to
its fate, or to its successor, seems to linger in the children's
song "London Bridge is broken down". Old London Bridge
was built of many arches, and supported a double row of timbered houses, and until 1739 it was the only crossing of the
river. Very few visitors to London can avoid standing for a
moment and looking down the river with its shipping, its cranes
and its wharves. Those that do unconsciously belong to a
"goodly company".

"And just as everybody who crosses it today peers over
for a moment to the business of ships below, so Herman
Melville, who wrote our greatest story of the sea (Moby
Dick), leaned on this parapet to consider the ships, the
morning he arrived in London" (*Below London Bridge* by
Tomlinson).

Straight ahead, as we cross the Bridge, under the railway
arch that links Charing Cross with the coast, lies the Borough,
and on the right, at a much lower level than the present street,
stands the Church of St. Saviour's or Southwark Cathedral.
This church was originally attached to the Augustine Priory
of St. Mary Overie. The American reader may be interested
to know that John Harvard was baptized here on November
29th 1607. The church contains a memorial to Shakespeare,
and the Globe theatre was situated immediately behind the
cathedral.

"The original foundation of London Bridge, by report of
Bartholomew Linstead, last Prior of St. Mary Overies
church of Southwark, was this:

A ferry being kept in place where now the bridge is built,
at length the ferryman and his wife deceasing, left the
same to their daughter, a maiden named Mary, which with
the goods and profits arising, built a house of Sisters ...
after converted into a college ... the priest built the bridge
of timber ... till at length ... by the aid of the citizens of
London, and others a bridge was built with arches of stone"
(John Stow).

Although our way leads down Duke Street Hill to Tooley
Street, we will just pause a moment, for the Borough High
Street teems with interest. Adjoining the cathedral is Borough
Market and close by is Clink Street, famous or infamous, in-
asmuch as a prison stood here originally for the confinement

of heretics, and the word "clink" has passed into thieves'
slang as a synonym for prison. Further along the High Street
another prison was situated known as the Marshalsea, used
from 1377 until 1842 first for political prisoners, and later
for debtors, in which the father of Charles Dickens was imprisoned for debt.

Southwark
Cathedral

Coaches from Dover and the south could travel no further
than the Borough as the Bridge was too narrow for them to
pass. Consequently the High Street was a street of Inns.

Geffrey Chaucer speaks of the Tabard Inn, in his Canterbury Tales:

"Befell that in that season, on a day
In Southwark at the Tabard, as I lay,
Readie to wenden on my pilgrimage
To Canterburie with devout courage,
At night was come into the hosterie
Well nine and twentie in a companie".

The Tabard was so called by the sign, which was, as we now term it, a jacket, or sleeveless coat ... a stately garment of old time, commonly worn by noblemen.

"In the Borough there still remain some half-dozen old inns which have preserved their external features unchanged, and which have escaped alike the rage of public improvement and the encroachments of private speculation. Great rambling queer old places with galleries passages and staircases wide enough and antiquated enough to furnish material for a hundred ghost stories"(*Pickwick* Dickens). Since Dickens wrote these words, only one old galleried inn remains, the George, with one balconied section intact. The old High Street, before it was cleared away in 1830 was reputed to be the narrowest leading into the centre of London. Dickens is remembered also in the Church of St. George's, in the Borough, called also "The church of Little Dorrit".

Little Dorrit's Church.

"Strange isn't it, how much of real London still lies South of the river, just as it did in Shakespeare's day, and in Chaucer's day before him? It is as though across the Thames - in London's Deep South - times and manners have not changed so much as in the Parliamentary North" (Norman Collins).

However fascinating this ramble may be, we must exercise restraint, retrace our steps and at the foot of London Bridge

turn left and make our way along Tooley Street to Horsleydown,
Bermondsey. "Tooley Street", a corruption of "St. Olave's
Street" is a street of warehouses, wharf entrances and some-
what poor dwellings. To quote the author of *Below London Bridge*

"Funny smells here ... yes distinctly curious! A funny
blended odour of the wood and straw of boxes of eggs, and
of tea, cheese, butter and bacon. It was merely Tooley
Street. Some people could name it blindfolded. You come
out of the smell of the Borough - and everyone knows the
whiff of hops - and in the street below, where begin the
paths that follow the south shore to Woolwich, the cargoes
to spread London's breakfast table are discharged. Soon
there were close above us sooty precipices of brickwork.
Now and then in these heights there were perforations, as
Hole-in-the-Wall, or Horsleydown Stairs. Here and there
(in times past) it was convenient to land amid sedges from
coracles and canoes. London has lasted longer than Tyre
and Sidon" (Tomlinson).

Horsley Down, Horseydown or Horsedown, adjoins Bermondsey Abbey Church, (see drawing on page 19) founded by Cluniac
Monks and was used as a pasture ground for the Horse Fair,
perpetuated in the name Fair Street, to which spot our steps
have all the while been directed. Tooley Street was made famous by a petition sent to the House of Commons by "three
tailors of Tooley Street" who opened their petition with the
proud words "We the People of England" - no keeping a Bermondsey boy down evidently / The chief industries of Bermondsey were, and perhaps are, leather and the docks, with all the
adjuncts of lightermen, stevedors and pilots. We had a saying,

    "Scotland has men of Ayr,
    Ireland men of Cork,
    But London has "Lightermen"!

A walk along Bermondsey wall would pass "Quays that could
have mounds of coco-nuts, chests of tea built as high as
houses, black pools of molasses ... hogsheads of sugar".

    "It is no good pretending that coal wharves, guano factories
    and Bathing Creek, though socially necessary, are common-
    ly edifying. They are glum, and if the wind is in the wrong
    quarter you wish you were not there" (Tomlinson).

The reason why Horsleydown becomes the Mecca of this pilgrimage is simply that I was born there.

The priory of St. Saviour's was called "Bermond's Eye" and was founded by Alwin Childe in 1081. Upon the decease of Alwin in 1094 William Rufus gave to the monks his manor of Bermondsey, and built for them a new great church. In after years, the church of St. Mary Magdalene was built by the priors of Bermondsey, which is now the parish church, and in which Dr. Bullinger as a young man was Curate.

Dr. Bullinger in his monumental work, *"Figures of Speech used in the Bible"*, refers to others who had explored the subject before him, and among them mentions Benjamin Keach (1640/1704) and his book *"Troposchemalogia; or a key to open the Scripture metaphors and types"*. Another work by this author is entitled *"The Jewish Sabbath Abrogated"*, which shows the trend of his thoughts. Keach was the minister of the oldest non-conformist Chapel in Bermondsey, and it was situated in Horsleydown. Two doors East of the churchyard of St. John's, Horsleydown in Fair Street, and possibly in the house in which I was born, Thomas Guy, the founder of Guy's Hospital, was born in the year 1645. Two hundred and thirty-six years after, in 1881, Guy's Hospital was instrumental in saving my life after a severe burn, the scars of which mark my body until this day.

Owing to a minor industrial crisis, the whole of my parents' possessions were stacked into the one room they then rented, and into that very lowly home I made my entry on April 25th in the year 1880. At that time my father was a follower of Bradlaugh the atheist, and was also an ardent advocate for "free education" which did not become law for some years after.

The influence of Bradlaugh necessarily meant that as a family we lived "without God". Honest as the day, kindly as the summer sun, and with a sense of liberty that was in some things in advance of the times, my parents were all that a boy could wish, except for the fact, though I realised it not at the time, that the Bible was never opened and its message entirely unknown. I remember once picking up a book and opening it at random, but seeing that it dealt with Christian themes, with something like a sense of guilt at even glimpsing at such a book, I put it down as a work with which I could have neither part or lot. That book was *"The Pilgrim's Progress"* by John Bunyan. What the effect would have been had I read it, and come under its sway is but an empty speculation. The Lord had His own way and time when He would

lead me to see my need of a Saviour, and in view of His ulti-
mate purposes, His time is always best.

I grew up therefore in entire ignorance both of the Word
and of its Gospel message. I do remember wishing that a
teacher at school had not explained the Lord's Prayer in the
light of the added verse, Matthew 6:14, for it seemed to give
the other boy a somewhat unfair advantage in the interminable
schoolboy quarrels that arose, but apart from this, and some
outlandish names from the books of Chronicles and Kings,
the Bible was a closed book to me.

St. John's
Horsleydown

Reference to St. John's Church is on page 13

In order better to appreciate the grace manifested to me, it will be necessary to go back to the birthplace, South of the Thames. From the approach to the Tower Bridge, the main thoroughfare, Tooley Street extends Westward to London Bridge, and Eastward to Greenwich. (see map on end paper) Some ten minutes' walk from the place of my birth was a district made famous or infamous by Charles Dickens in his novel *"Oliver Twist"*. It was known as Jacob's Island, and although much had been done to rid the neighbourhood of the tragic evils that existed when Dickens wrote of it, it still remained a sore spot in the vicinity.

All that is left of St. John's Church is an empty shell, the two houses and the church being destroyed in air raids.

Toward the latter part of the eighteenth century, an attempt was made to make Bermondsey a fashionable watering place. In 1770 a chalybeate spring was discovered near Grange Road, which fact is still perpetuated in the name Spa Road, but there is nothing salubrious about that neighbourhood now.

❖❖❖❖❖❖❖

OF THE STOCK OF DEVON

The Apostle could write of himself "Of the stock of Israel" but I am a Gentile and only allude to Paul's reference to his forefathers as a heading, for we must leave the birthplace of the present writer, to get some inkling of his forbears. Unlike Israel, I can only go back four generations. The Apostle knew who were his "fathers", but the average Gentile can trace his ancestry back no further than a few generations. My father's people were Exeter folk, and I can go back as far as my father's grandfather, but have never pursued the matter further. My name "Welch" is a variant of the spelling "Welsh" but apart from the fact that Devonshire is near to Wales, I have no evidence that any of my forefathers hailed from the Principality. The word "Welch" was used by the Saxon invaders of this island as a label for the inhabitants of Britain and meant a "foreigner". It seems fitting, that one who was to be used in making known the exceeding riches of His grace to those who were by nature "strangers and foreigners" should himself bear a name meaning "foreigner". It may be that it is quite accidental - but then so might have been the naming of Saul of Tarsus by the Gentile name "Paul", but it is significant nevertheless. While my forefathers for several generations at least were Devonshire folk, I myself was born in London. My great grandfather appears to have been of a more sturdy build than I, as his portrait, reproduced further on, will show. I know little of my great grandmother except that she rather coddled her son, my grandfather, much to his undoing however, for I understand he was rather a gay lad and often came home the worse for his night out.

There are two incidents that I feel worth recording about my great grandfather which, though not on a high spiritual plane, nevertheless reveal some integrity of character.

Built 1593   The Guild Hall
                Exeter.

In a street just off the High Street, now alas bombed and rebuilt, and just opposite the ancient Guild Hall, my great grandfather, John Welch, ran what would have been an equivalent to a garage to-day, horses, and not cars however being his care. One day a lady of the county called upon him and told him that her nephew was putting up for parliament, and said that she expected John to give him his vote. "But my lady", said John, "I am a liberal, and I shall vote liberal". There was no secret ballot it must be remembered in those days. "Well John" she replied, "You know what will happen if you do". John knew full well, and IT DID. She withdrew her patronage, her friends did likewise and John Welch's business failed. I am not concerned about political parties, but I am glad my forbear was not intimidated in a matter of conscience and integrity.

As a set off over against what might be misrepresenting him as of too stern a nature is the other incident. John Welch was in the habit of visiting the local inn to meet his cronies of an evening, and always took with him a clay pipe, with which he enforced his point of view, *but he never smoked in his life.* He could be both adamant to the extent of financial loss, and yet tolerant, where essentials were not involved. Great grandfather's vote and clay pipe stood for something. Before the collapse of John's business, it seems that my grandfather, his son, was in the habit of going to the tailors, ordering a suit, and having the bill sent to his father. The only time my father, his grandson as a boy, heard a bad word from his grandfather's lips, was on these occasions, when upon receiving yet another unpaid bill he said "damn it!"

My grandmother on my father's side was a lady of Quaker stock, and as a boy, my father lived during his first few years in Orchard Place, Heavitree, Exeter, but at the time of the opening of the great exhibition in Hyde Park, the little family came to London, and my grandfather obtained employment in Kent's brush making factory, which was then in Tabard Street, a street associated as it always will be with Chaucer's Canterbury Pilgrims. I can still conjure up in the mind's eye, the odd mixture he presented, of past better days and of present straitened conditions. He would go off to work wearing a silk hat, a rather green frock coat, and a white bibbed apron tied round his waist! He was over six feet tall, wore "dundreary whiskers" and had an eye like an hawk. Owing to his upbringing, or rather to his lack of responsibility in the use of money, his family were often reduced to the verge of poverty, for a whole week's wages would sometimes be entirely spent in treating anyone and everyone to drink.

I remember that my grandfather used a "Boot-Jack" which had come with him from Exeter. Again, quoting Dickens in Little Dorrit:

"You have had a long walk, and will be glad to get your boots off. As to Daniel here, I suppose he'd never think of taking *his* boots off, unless we showed him a boot-jack".

Perhaps it is not to be wondered at that my father was never very robust, yet, although he suffered with intermittent haemorrhage of the lungs, he lived within a few months of ninety years of age. Among the industries of Bermondsey, owing to the vast amount of shipping, hemp ropes were in constant demand, and several rope walks were in the vicinity of Jamaica Road. The introduction of steel ropes brought the hemp rope making to a standstill, and my father fell out of employment. In those days there was no provision to aid such, and a desperate situation had to be faced, and here the stirling character of my mother came into play. She had an ingrained horror of debt; hire purchase and its equivalents were to her anathema, and so my parents left their little house and took one room in the house in Fair Street, and there, with all the furniture they possessed stacked, I was born on April 25th 1880. A somewhat indigent student from Guy's Hospital brought me into the world, and was glad to share the frugal Sunday dinner that was ready. As soon as I could be left with my grandmother, my mother went back to her silk work in Wood Street, Cheapside, so that my father would be free to make a fresh start, which he did in the leather bag industry, starting at a nominal wage and rising to be the head of his department when he left at the age of 70.

My parents were married at Lambeth Parish Church, hard by the Lambeth Palace, which is about as near to the Arch-

Lambeth
Palace
& Parish Church

bishop as I can hope to come. My father went to his wedding by rowing boat.

A tablet affixed to the tower records that Brvan Tuberville

in the year 1711 left one hundred pounds for ever, the interest to be used in assisting the apprenticeship of poor boys of the neighbourhood, with a notice that reads:

"N. B.   None to be put to chimney sweeps ..."

Lambeth Palace which adjoins the Church has been the London residence of the Archbishops of Canterbury since the 13th Century.

The gatehouse entrance shown in the sketch was built in 1490 to take the place of an earlier one. Behind this gateway will be found two reminders of early reformers namely, the Lollard's Tower and the Lollard's Prison. Queen Elizabeth's favourite, Essex, was imprisoned here in 1601.

Something of the character of the days of my childhood can be gathered from the following extract from the *Times* for April 7th, 1880, which speaks of an action against a shipowner at Sierra Leone for being engaged in slave trade; an advertisement for a second and third school master for Brentwood at a salary of £45 and £40 per annum, a reference to General Garibaldi, to Renan, to Sims Reeve a well known singer, to Moore and Burgess Minstrels, to Henry Irving and Ellen Terry and to "What Mr. Gladstone said" in Linlithgow!

In the portrait section a photograph shows my mother holding me as a babe of thirteen months, dressed up like an alderman, but innocent then of any problem of "Right Division"! Two months later I was badly scalded, and rushed off to Guy's hospital, where small hopes of recovery were held out. However, after three months treatment I left the hospital, but needing much attention. While in the hospital, the surgeon suggested that my mother be willing to have a portion of skin removed from her body and used to promote the healing of the wound. However, as another child was on its way, my father stepped in, but was met by an Irish nurse with her arm in a sling, who had already volunteered!

Skin grafting, as it is known to-day, was not practised in 1880, but the surgeon was evidently feeling out towards it. I of course can remember nothing of all this, being only eighteen months old when discharged, but one cannot help but be grateful for the bravery and the kindness shown to a tiny mite; nor can one quite still the feeling that a foreknown earthen vessel was preserved though scarred for life.

Guy's Hospital, which under God, saved my life, lies behind London Bridge Station, and the tall tower shown here is a well known land mark. The hospital owes its foundation to Thomas Guy, born in 1645, who lived in Fair Street, Horsleydown, and who left £200,000 endowment to the hospital. When

C

I was born, no one possessing 200,000 pence would have chosen Fair Street as a suitable dwelling place. The east wing of the hospital was destroyed in the blitz of 1940.

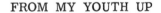

FROM MY YOUTH UP

Guy's
Hospital

Although the Apostle Paul attributed his whole Christian life and ministry to divine grace, he nevertheless makes many references to his upbringing. Lessons are drawn from his schooling, his Roman citizenship and other details, for while inspiration is all of God, nevertheless it is written "The Holy Ghost *by the mouth* of David spake", the earthen vessel not being set aside but taken up and used.

When my mother held her infant son out of the window over the open space around St. John's Church, Horsleydown,* to induce sleep in a very wide-awake youngster, he was not so wide-awake and beyond his years to know or to note that, from that point of vantage he might have seen across the housetops the tower of Bermondsey Abbey Church, famous in earlier days for providing sanctuary to more than one Royal Personage, but interesting to us, for the fact that some years earlier Ethelbert W. Bullinger, later to be known and loved as Dr. Bullinger, acted in this church as curate. Neither my parents nor the beloved Doctor knew that the paths thus unconsciously crossed, geographically speaking, were destined to be blessedly associated in spiritual things some years later. *see page 12

Tooley Street, about which we have already spoken ends at Dockhead and then becomes Jamaica Road. A glance at the map which forms the end paper of the cover, shows not only these names, but the following streets and buildings that now

Bermondsey Abbey Church
(see page 10)

come into the picture. Flockton Street, Drummond Road, Cherry Garden Pier, Keeton's Road, and Jamaica Road, Herold's School, Keeton's Road School, The Bermondsey Settlement, Peek Frean's Biscuit Works and the Drummond Road Baptist Chapel.

"Jamaica Road, which lost many of its houses in the blitz of May 1941, is so called from an inn called the Jamaica,

which once stood in the immediate locality. Three years
later, on 15th June, 1944, Numbers 123-69 of Jamaica Road,
including "Roses's Chapel" were completely destroyed by a
flying bomb ... On the south side of Jamaica Road, at the
northern end of Spa Road, is St. James's Church, a spacious
building of brick and stone in the Greek style erected in
1829"

The Face of London Harold P. Clunn.

Jamaica Road was so badly hit in the blitz that I could not
verify the site of many of the shops with which I had grown
familiar. At the corner of Drummond Road stood Reason's
the corn chandlers, with an intriguing smell of cattle and
poultry food and spice, Next there was an old fashioned tobac-
conist with a display of snuff, and then a fishmongers, and
then "Bonny the Butcher", a cut above our purse. After this
came Cownley's, kept by two elderly ladies who might have
stepped out of Cranford, and where coloured rainbow wool
could be bought and made into coloured reins for playing at
horses. Next came Davis's cheesemongers and after a tea
grocers, and a hat shop, came Merrils the furniture store,
spoken about on page 38

On the opposite side of the road was Jones the tea grocers
which advertised itself by a huge red tea pot on the parapet.
Here I did the week's shopping for my mother. One regular
item was "an ounce of two shilling Green Tea", which was always weighed meticulously in a pair of balances suspended
from the ceiling.

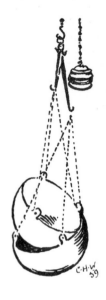

In that second raid, both Herold's
School (infants' department) and the
row of houses including 20 Drummond Road, to which we had moved in
1884, were reduced to rubble. Mention has been made of St. James's
Church. I remember taking one of
my daughters, as a child to show her
the slide which the children of the
neighbourhood improvised out of the
granite slabs that bordered the steps
leading into the church. These slabs
still retain the polish that countless
breeches' seats were worn out to ac-
complish, but to my surprise I discovered that even here the old order had
given place to new, for there, standing in the grounds and rendering the
granite slides obsolete, was a grand
structure - tobogganing made easy in

all weathers. Both ancient and modern "slides" have been
indicated in the accompanying sketch.

There were some rather coarse comments on Saturday
nights when the carillon of St. James's rang out the tune

"There is no luck about the house
Since my old man's away"

Ancient & Modern
Slides at
St James's.

C·H·W
/59

for alas! A staggering drunken man was no uncommon sight
in those early days, and on Saturday nights in particular.
At that time we youngsters had no ideas as to good or bad
architecture but the following extracts from an article in the
Daily Telegraph   may be worth preserving.

St, James Church, in Jamaica Road, Bermondsey, one of
the best examples of the 19th century architecture of Savage, is in danger of demolition.
John Betjeman,   The Daily Telegr aph Architectural Correspondent writes:

St. James's, Bermondsey, was designed and built by James
Savage, in 1827-29. It is a grand building on a prominent
site in a wide churchyard.   It was built of London stock
brick with a Bath stone steeple surmounted by an enormous
dragon as weathervane.

Outside, the church owes much to Vanbrugh, with its solemn
blind arches and entrance front. It cost £21,000 to build,
a lot of money in that time and half of it subscribed by the
people of Bermondsey.

Cherry Garden
Pier.

From 1884 until 1904, 20 Drummond Road was my centre, and the surrounding streets, including Dockland and South- wark Park, were my environment. It will be observed that Jamaica Road runs parallel with the river and separated the district into two parts, those running down to the river being exceedingly poor and squalid, and inextricably mixed up with wharves, docks, piers and smells. Cherry Garden Pier was only about five minutes walk from Drummond Road, but to a young boy at that time, a journey fraught with adventure and sometimes with danger. The name conjures up white blossom, orchards, Pleasure Gardens and the like, even as Vauxhall was a place of resort and pleasure from the days of Charles ll until abolished in 1859, but Cherry Gardens was now only a name. While in a most unprepossessing neighbourhood, Cherry Garden Pier is in constant use; on page 22 the sketch gives some idea of the pier and foreshore.

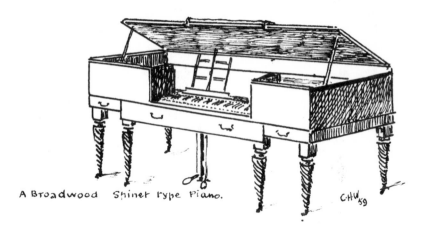

A Broadwood   Spinet Type Piano.   C.H.U.59

Before proceeding further, I must hark back two years to join up with a later link in the narrative and give a word about Flockton Street. While it is shown on the map immediately behind Dockhead, the only trace I could find of its whereabouts were the curb stones that had resisted the blitz which wiped out this river-side turning. Flockton Street links up with two later events which, though out of order, can best be introduced here. At the age of six, see photograph on page 88, I started having piano lessons practising on a spinet shaped Broadwood piano, with a very restricted keyboard. Such pieces as "The blue bells of Scotland", or "The Fairy wedding Waltz" were about the zenith of this first musical adventure.

Occasionally we children anticipated modern "Jazz" by

placing sheets of newspaper on the wires and creating a tinny banjo effect!

Later in life I came to appreciate the three great "B's" of music, Bach, Beethoven and Brahms. Whether others appreciated my attempts is a moot point!

Dr. Bullinger was no mean musician, one of his best known hymn tunes being set to the words "I am trusting Thee Lord Jesus". Though musical, he stood firmly against the so-called musical services. Whilst not posing as a musician I am thankful that at a pinch I can step in and play either the organ or piano, and can also produce some weird noises on both the violin and the "cello".

My mother like most of her class and day, had very little schooling, but it was manifest that she had an innate love for both music and drawing. When first married and before any children claimed her care, she used to lean over the bannisters on the top floor while the landlady's daughter had her music lesson below, and then, when the teacher had left my mother would use the same instruction book and go over the lesson as far as possible.

"Ancient Lights" C·H·W·59

I can remember so well sitting on Sunday evening with my mother while we both attempted to draw the intricate Greek fret pattern on the frosted glass shade of the parlour lamp. This reminds me of one effort at artistic expression that did NOT receive parental approbation. My mother found me sitting on the pavement outside the house endeavouring to emulate the "pavement artist", with his Mackerel, Sunsets, Dogs heads and some such appealing slogan as: "One Shower of rain, my work is all in vain".

The reference to the parlour lamp makes me realise that I have lived through a wonderful evolution of lighting, from the crude hanging wall lamp, the squeaking fish-tail gas light, the incandescent burner, the arc light, electric filament lamp, and the neon light.

When ten, I became a chorister at Christ Church, Bermondsey,
wearing a surplice, singing the Psalms, Hymns and Anthems,
but having not the slightest knowledge of the way of salvation,
nor even being conscious that I needed a Saviour. Once, and
only once, I, together with the massed choirs of many churches, sang in St. Paul's Cathedral, but no interviewer singled
me out as a juvenile Caruso! Music without Christ is the tag
I place on this period, for in the same neighbourhood a few

Christ Church Bermondsey
Percy Hall.

years later music and Christian service could be the changed
slogan. The accompanying drawing shows two buildings, the
Church in the foreground, and the Bermondsey Gospel Mission then called "Percy Hall" in the rear.

Now to return to Flockton Street. In 1882 this mission used to hold open air meetings in the surrounding neighbourhood, and as a child of two I used to join in singing the hymn "Whiter than the snow" with an eye I suspect on the old lady who kept the sweet shop, who would exclaim "Bless his little heart" and add to the spoken blessing a screw of sweets! When at the age of 72 I spoke at a meeting at the Bermondsey Gospel Mission and told them that my *first active fellowship* with the mission was 70 years earlier, I could see some bewildered mental arithmetic proceeding.

Anticipating yet another few years, to a period immediately following my conversion, I was invited to share with another young man in the work of visiting local Sunday Schools in the interest of The "Regions Beyond" Missionary movement. Upon objecting "I could never speak at a meeting" the rejoinder was "You come. If the Lord has work for you to do, you will find it waiting for you". Sure enough, an agitated superintendent button-holed me on the doorstep with the question, "Can you play the organ?" I did not know. I could play the piano - but feeling here was the "work waiting" I pulled out several stops at random, hoped for the best, and found this time that the musical association was combined most definitely with the Gospel. Although it is evident that a love of music was ingrained, music has never been permitted to have much place in my ministry. It can often be a snare.

We must now turn back, as this digression has taken us forward some twenty years. At one end of Drummond Road, where it joins Jamaica Road, were the Herold Schools, which at the time occupied a site on either side of the road. The infants' department was flattened in a raid, but the upper school is still represented by the Herold's Institute.

Between 1884 and 1885, that is between the age of four and five years, I attended a private school, but learned practically nothing, and I believe that my comment was that it was "soppy"! I was then sent to Herold's Infant School where I remained for about a year. Owing to the many scrapes I got into even at that early age, my father provided me with a small diary in which the teacher was asked to write in the morning either the word "good" or "bad". The first day went off well, but alas the second afternoon was disfigured by the word "bad"! I remember at the age of five standing outside the house trying to alter the word "bad" to "good" an experiment in accommodating theology and textual criticism which I discovered did not work. When my parents discovered to their horror that I had taken "a dare", and had started doing a "strip tease" in front of the class, they concluded that it was no use keeping me at such "respectable" institutions, but that I must go

to the Board School, where discipline exercised both by
scholar and teacher might have some rewarding effect. So at
the age of six I entered Keeton's Road School, and remained
there until the age of fourteen, when I reached the Ex. VIIth
standard, the highest in a school of that type. Some four years
after, a little girl named Winifred Jeannette Clark, who lived
right down on the water front became a pupil in Herold's In-

fant School, and later transferred to Keeton's Road School,
became the friend of my own sister Kit, and ultimately under
the good hand of the Lord, became the loving and loyal partner, help-meet and fellow sharer in the good fight of faith.

Two certificates for Scripture knowledge, dated 1887 and
1888, show that at the age of seven and eight I had become acquainted with the letter of the Word, but still wonder why the
authorities feel that such passages as "Blessed are ye, when

men shall revile you, and persecute you, and shall say all manner of evil against you falsely, for My Name's sake" should
be considered milk for babes. I certainly gained nothing spiritually from such exercises. Certificates for 2nd standard
1888, 3rd standard 1889, 4th in 1890 on to 7th and Ex. 7th in
1893, accompanied with a certificate for Alternative Elementary Physics at the age of twelve, Mechanics, Drawing, and
French in 1893 at the age of thirteen, give some idea of the
progress made and the nature of the teaching given. George
E. Powell was an old fashioned Head Master, who had wisdom
enough however to give younger teachers a fairly free hand.
It was his custom to put all boys who were down for punishment into a line, and go along the line with a mock solemnity,
saying with each cut of the cane "miserable sinner"! "miserable sinner".
A school chant at the time revealed no disrespect however as
we sang:

> "Mr. Powell's a nice old man. He tries to teach us
>   all he can,
>   Reading, Writing and Arithmetic, but he doesn't forget
>   to give us the stick.
>   When he does, he makes us dance, out of England
>   into France,
>   Out of France into Spain; all round the world
>   and back again".

At the annual prize giving in 1889, when I was just turned
nine years old, a "Queen Victoria Medal" was pinned on my
breast. I had, quite by accident not been late or absent from
school for a year.

Punctuality — "The courtesy
        of Kings"

This was repeated for three succeeding years, the fourth being marked by a special medal in bronze. Someone said,
four consecutive years without being late or absent once, was

not only a credit to the youngster but to his mother, especially where there were younger members of a large family to be
cared for.

Those who are in the habit of attending the meetings at the
Chapel of the Opened Book, have no need to look anxiously at
the clock. It is as dishonest to steal a person's time as his
money. Little souls sometimes adopt Malvolio's idea of great-
ness:

"I frown the while, and perchance wind up my watch, or
play with some rich jewel" but
"Punctuality is the courtesy of kings".

see page 30

Keerons Rd.
L.C.C. School.

C.H.W.
'59.

Memory is a strange thing, and it is difficult to understand
where and how happenings of seventy years ago can be called
to mind without effort. I can repeat without hesitation the
names on the register in the class when I was eight years old.

There is an hiatus where day dreaming took the place of vigilance, but as my name came last in alphabetical order, all was well. Here is the list:-

Bilbee, Butler, Beresford, Breeze, Culling, Cosh, Dunlop, Elms, Fleming, Gale, Hogg, Humphries, Joy, May . . . . Walker, Walling, Welch.

To W. H. Tulk must go the credit for keeping the school up to date in the matter of Science. In 1894 at this L. C. C. School (as it had become) I was initiated into the wonders of Spectrum Analysis, Newton's Disc, Photo-Synthesis, Sound, Light, Heat, Magnetism and Electricity, and have been surprised in after life to meet men who on the surface had received far better training than I, but who had not had so clear a conception of these elements of scientific research as had then been part of the ordinary syllabus at Keeton's Road School.

The playground of the boys' section was partly open and partly covered, the building above being supported on rows of pillars. The Surrey Docks was naturally a target for enemy bombers, and in 1940 or thereabouts, about two hundred rendered homeless by such an attack were shepherded down to take shelter in the covered playground of the school. That night a direct hit on the school buried that two hundred souls, and not one, so far as I can discover, escaped. One wing of the school still functions, but the school I knew as a boy is no more. The picture on page 29 drawn in January 1959 shows the condition of the building that remains.

In 1894 when I was fourteen I left school and sought some form of employment. In after years, when my parents were not so hard pressed, it was possible to give two of my younger sisters a college training, but although I longed for further and richer training, that at the time was out of the question. I then answered an advertisement for "an intelligent lad" and entered a Tea Broker's establishment in Rood Lane, E. C., and there for a year I ate my heart out, much as Dickens did in the Blacking Factory, for I hated as many boys did the homely chores that an eldest child perforce had to share. Here, "someone in the city" to his shame, spent most of his time battling with a never ending mountain of china cups and pots used by the tea-tasters of the firm.

Occasionally I paid a visit to such wharves as Butler's, Hay's, or St. Katharines, but revolted at the age of fifteen, gave up the princely salary of five shillings a week, and was out of employment for six or seven weeks, baffled but unbowed.

Here I must again break the chronological sequence. At the age of twenty five, that is ten years after being dismissed from

Rood Lane, I was conducting a party around the British Museum, and had been explaining some of the exhibits seen in the Egyptian Room. As was always a possibility, a member of the public drew near and joined the party. At a halt in the lecture I turned to him and said "You evidently are interested". He replied "I am indeed". I added "You do not recognize me?" In astonishment he said "No". I slipped into the Cockney vernacular, saying "You gave me the sack ten years ago". He was the Secretary of the firm and rejoiced at such a transformation. Time's Revenges need not always be saddening. Of course a radical change had come about in those intervening ten years, to which all the incidents of this narrative are all the while converging.

As no opening had seemed to be forthcoming, my father who was himself in the Leather Bag industry, said I had better take up the same craft, and so, when I was fifteen I started at Wolfsky & Co., Leather bag makers, with whom I stayed, apart from about two years at Seefel's in Barbican and Jacobs in Wilson Street, until I left at the age of twenty four to take up the Secretaryship of a Bible Training College.

Whether we be blue blooded aristocrats, or the lowest of classless serfs, our pedigree at last leads us back to the "one man" through whom "sin entered into the world"; the clay out of which God fashions vessels for His service is the same in every case.

Upbringing and environment are the instruments used in the shaping of these vessels, and in particular the influences of parent, home and school during the impressionable years of early youth.

By nature a child is provided with two parents, but modern life often robs him of the balancing care of the father; a mother's love is immediate and protective, a father's looks to the future and is corrective. Happy is the child who has both. It should be remembered that the Scripture says "Fathers" not "Mothers"bring up your children in the nurture and admonition of the Lord. (Eph. 6:4; Cor. 3:21; Heb. 12:5-12).

My father used to leave home each morning about 7 a.m. and we children still in our beds would hear the little ritual that was unfailingly observed.

"Good-bye Mum. I'm off".

"Good-bye. Have you got your bag Dad?"

"Yes my dear".

Dad would walk to Spa Road station (now demolished) and take either a penny fare to London Bridge, or if extra weary, a three halfpenny fare to Cannon Street station, and then walk

through to Old Street where he was employed. We saw no more
of Dad until eight o'clock at night, and those still young would
by then have gone to bed.

Looking back over the years with a sympathetic understanding which only time could bring, I can see that in his own quiet
way, my father exercised an influence over his family of one
boy and six girls that was not immediately obvious. I doubt
whether he would have tried to give a definition of the word
"philosophy", and yet he had a simple nature, a wisdom that
knew no parade, and often with self depreciation he had marked influence on a growing child.

He would appreciate the rustic wit of Corin the shepherd in
As You Like It:

Touchstone   "Hast any philosophy in thee shepherd?"
Corin   "No more but that I know the more one sickens
                 the worse at ease he is: and that he that wants
                 money, means, and content is without three
                 good friends: that the property of rain is to
                 wet, and fire to burn; that good pasture makes
                 fat sheep, that a great cause of the night is
                 lack of sun: that he that hath learned no wit by
                 nature nor art may complain of good breeding
                 and comes of a very dull kindred".

As I have said elsewhere, I had no Christian upbringing.
The Scriptures were unknown, the Gospel and its blessings
like the language of a foreign land. Recognising all this, I
nevertheless cannot help but be grateful that my father did
according to his light, seek to play a father's part.

How many boys of twelve have been taken aside, and had the
advice of old Polonius read and explained to them? This passage is lacking in spiritual grace, yet for what it was worth,
think of the effect upon a schoolboy hearing for the first time
such counsel as:

"Look thou character. Give thy thoughts no tongue,
Nor any unproportion'd thought his act.
Be thou familiar, but by no means vulgar;
The friends thou hast, and their adoption tried,
Grapple to thy soul with hoops of steel;
But do not dull thy palm with entertainment
Of each new-hatched, unfledg'd comrade. Beware
Of entrance to a quarrel, but, being in
Bear't that th'opposed may beware of thee.
Give every man thine ear, but few thy voice:
Take each man's censure, but reserve thy judgment.

        . . . .

Neither a borrower, nor a lender be;
For loan oft loses both itself and friend,
And borrowing dulls the edge of husbandry
This above all: to thine own self be true,
And it must follow as the night the day,
Thou canst not then be false to any man".
On one occasion he drew me aside and said with purposed
mock solemnity:

"Boy, remember this. It's most unlucky to fall down and
break your neck ON WEDNESDAY".
By the time I had puzzled out this emphasis on Wednesday, I
could say with intent:

"It is not in our stars, but in ourselves that we are under-
lings".
My father also had a way of throwing into a conversation a
simple bit of proverbial wisdom. For example, when someone had been unduly stressing the obligation that the young
folk had to support their aged parents, he to their surprise,
said:

"Young sparrows don't save up to feed old sparrows" and
left it at that. Had such a proverb come from an undutiful son
or daughter it would have worn a different complexion.

Without enlarging on this influence on young outlook, here
are a few more samples of his rude yet very sane and kindly
philosophy.
When facing some adverse conditions that threatened our
peace as a family he might say.

"Oh well, we've never died in a winter yet"!
Or again at a time when he had hardly a penny to bless himself with he might spring a riddle like this on us:

"What is the difference between me and a millionaire?"
The answer was

"Well he has started on his SECOND million, I've only
started on my FIRST"!
Once at the tea table he caught us all napping by springing on
us the question:

"Who killed Cain?". We all yelled out "Abel"!

On page 8.2 is a drawing I made of my father when I was
about nineteen and he was about fifty one or two.

Two names were held in great respect in our home, and were
familiar in our mouths as household words, namely, Charles
Dickens, and William Ewart Gladstone, my father continuing
the Liberalism of his grandfather, of whom we have spoken
on page 14 . The fact that within five minutes walk there
was a "Ragged School" of about four hundred children, coupled

with the further fact that the street was our playground, and that many of the boys with whom I mixed were little blackguards, but emphasises the overshadowing grace of the Lord in those formative yet unspiritual days.

The streets of course were not so lined with traffic as they are today, and street sellers added a little to the otherwise drab surroundings.

An old man would come along in tattered clothing with a little white toy lamb fastened to the brim of his hat, singing in a cracked old voice:

"Young lambs to sell. Young lambs to sell.
If I'd as much money as I could tell
I would not be crying young lambs to sell".

Another with a basket on his arm, would walk along saying in a grumpy voice:

"All brown 'uns. All brown 'uns. Gravesend Shrimps.
All brown 'uns".

Insecticides were unknown, but one wearing an old top hat to which was fastened a sheet of sticky paper, would be heard calling:

"Catch 'em alive O"
"As through the streets Fly
Papers I cry
The boys holloa after me, bother your eye.
Catch 'em alive O".

In *Little Dorrit* Dickens, speaking about some old pictures, says: "Such coats of varnish that every holy personage served as a fly-trap, and became what is now called in the vulgar tongue a Catch-em-alive O".

On May Day the streets would be festive and colourful as "Jack in the Green" paraded the streets.

The name "Jack" occurs in many traditional settings:
Jack and Jill.
Jack the giant killer.
Jack and the beanstalk.
Jack Horner.
Jack Sprat.

Jack in the Green was a public holiday, also called "Chimney Sweepers' Day". It appears to have been a remnant of the

many sports and pastimes with which old London was enliven-
ed, and brought a touch of carnival into the lives of some that
were as dingy as the chimney sweep's.

The sweeps coloured their faces for a change with brickdust,
trimmed their hats with gilt paper, and one of their number
danced and capered inside a cone of evergreen.

In 1842 and again in 1864, acts of Parliament made the employment of "climbing boys" as they were called, illegal.
Charles Kingsley in the "Water Babies" speaks of these climb-
boys. To these, the tablet referred to on page 16 alludes,
when it forbad the apprenticing of boys to "chimney sweeps".

On May Day in the morning, folk would walk in the green
meadows and woods. There would be Maypole dancing and:
"Divers warlike shows, with good archers, Morris dan-
cers, and other devices for pastime all day long, and
toward the evening they had stage plays, and bonfires in
the streets".

A familiar cry was "A lot for ha'penny water cress" or as it
was usually pronounced "water creases". A mission that was
held under the railway arches of Spa Road Station stipulated
that no one could be a member of the mission band who did
not refrain from buying "water creases" on Sundays!

Another old chap would cry as he walked in from the surrounding country:
"Any chick weed and groundsel
for your singing bird-ies".

Yet another would peddle from door to door greeny grey lumps of hearth stone used for whitening door steps and hearths. Being the eldest I was roped in at times to use this hearth stone and clean the front door step. As I did not want any of the boys to see me doing "women's work" I knelt in the passage and

hung nearly upside down to do this chore. When cleaning the knives in those days with brick-dust I sometimes asked "who invented work", but at the time was ignorant of the reason for its irksomeness. There was no stainless steel at that time.

However we strike a pleasanter note as we remember the song:
"Sixteen branches a penny
Sweet lavender.
I will sell you sixteen branches
for a penny
All in bloom'.'
Again there was something approaching the romantic to hear on a misty November evening the tinkle of the bell of the muffin man.

Another relic of old times persisted in the recurring period when we built a grotto in the curb. This was made of coloured paper, a lighted candle and small stones and oyster shells. We had no idea that this was perpetuating a memory of pilgrimages, or that the oyster shells had any connexion with St. James. After building the grotto a boy would take an oyster shell, and keeping pace with a passer by, would chant:
"Please remember the grotto, only once a year.
Father's gone to sea, Mother's gone to fetch him back,
Please remember me".

I noticed that many a passer-by who contributed his penny never even saw the grotto that had been so carefully erected, and this gave me a brain-wave. Retiring to another street, I built no grotto, but chanted the prescribed words and collected fourpence halfpenny. My financial experiment however, horrified my mother at my duplicity, and so perhaps a financial wizard was lost to the City!

I have been driven in a Cadillac and the seventy miles an hour seemed but thirty. I can remember much more primitive ways of travel however. One was a one-horse bus that left St. James' Church. The passenger climbed aboard, put

his penny in a glass covered box which was visible to the driver, and when all were seated he pulled a cord and away we went with a gentle clip-clop, no petrol, no honking, no hurry. What bad old times! Fancy, no zebra crossings, no stop and go signals. Soon, with atomic energy and space travel we shall realise the experience predicted of the pilot who:

"Went out in a relative way
And came home the evening before"!

If, as I have indicated, I owe much to the unobtrusive guidance of my father, I am equally indebted to the example and care of my mother. From her I have inherited a horror of debt, her example supplementing the advice of old Polonius already quoted. Father was easy going but mother was an organizer, and both were happy in their spheres.

Although I was the eldest of the family, and the only son at that, there was never any favouritism shown. Mother distributed her love and care as well as her correction with an even hand, which if I did not appreciate at the time I have done so many times since.

For many years it fell to my lot to accompany my mother on her Saturday night shopping, and from her attitude in these transactions I derived much help.

One happening I place beside the story of Barrie's mother when she became the proud possessor of six horse hair bottomed chairs, as he recounts in his book *Margaret Ogilvie*. For many weeks, if not months, my mother would stand outside the furniture stores in Jamaica Road, but what was passing through her mind she told no one. At last however it was revealed, when a furniture van delivered a bed-room suite paid for in cash. Up till then a box covered with dimity over pink cotton, with a small swing mirror sufficed, but when at last this transformation was achieved what a day that was! We children were happy to have bare boards for a floor and blue washed walls. Mother bless her, was now housed like a Queen.

Another light upon her character is associated with the annual holiday which would never have been but for her careful budgetting. When the time drew near for arrangements to be made, I usually got time off from daily work and we went both of us together, mother and son, to Ramsgate, Hastings or some sea-side place to decide on the apartments that must be booked in advance. I learned to anticipate the procedure.

Armed with a number of addresses, her first move was to "look at their curtains". If the outside inspection was not satisfactory she would pass on to the next address until that test was passed. After coming to terms her next move was to visit the shopping centre where she would make a sort of slide rule. "That tin of apricots is a halfpenny more than at home, that cut of beef is a penny more" and so on.

In those days no respectable family allowed sweethearts to go off on holiday together, and so mother very diplomatically catered for her own family and for any associates, which worked out happily for all.

There was one Victorian attitude that I undertook to circumvent although my sisters feared that I would not succeed. I was going to get mother to consent (hold your breath) to MIXED BATHING. After much coaxing she consented to sit like Britannia in the middle of a curve in the beach, while father, who enjoyed the joke, fixed up a sheet with large stones over a depression in the cliff face. There the "girls" all undressed while the "boys" did the best they could at a distance. All went "swimmingly" until the time came to dress, and then we remembered the experience of King Canute. The tide had washed away the sheet, and there was nothing for it but that Dad and I had to wade in and rescue heaps of underclothing, dump them down at mother's feet and we all got dressed under her eye. But it was rare fun in which she entered as heartily as the youngest of us.

When the time came for me to make the great decision and give up a craft with an assured wage to take on an unspecified "Christian service" mother was not at all comfortable. She assured me that the people to whom I was going would take advantage of me, and some of her fears I must confess were realized, although these good folk had assured her that they would treat me "as though I were a son".

However that is all over and past; the good remains and the meanness is forgotten.

❖❖❖❖❖❖   ❖❖❖❖❖❖

The Apostle Paul, so far as we can gather from his writings, was a man of culture, and up to the time of his conversion, a man of independent means. He had, however, been taught a trade, in accordance with Hebrew custom, and was a "tent maker". Opinions differ as to whether this trade involved the process of weaving or not, but Chrysostom has no hesitation in speaking of the Apostle, after witnessing for the truth in bazaar and market, "sewing together skins of leather" while demons trembled and angels marvelled. Bermondsey at the time of my boyhood had a world wide reputation for "leather", and it is not therefore strange that I too should find myself engaged in a craft in which the Apostle himself could have taken an intelligent interest. I passed through the various phases of the craft, from the most delicate pocket book work to the heaviest hand sewn type, and to this day, I value the balance that an ability to work with one's hands, gives to anyone who is engaged in purely literary activities. Both the mighty Paul and his humble follower would say "these hands have ministered unto my necessities".

Leather
Craft

One of the strange things in the wheel of time is, that at the age of eighteen I worked at the leather bag makers, Jacobs & Sons, which is immediately opposite to the Chapel of the Opened Book, but in that period I was so lacking in interest concerning things spiritual, that I have no recollection of *ever seeing* that a Chapel stood there. Now my name can be read on the Chapel notice board from the very window at which I worked.

About this time I must have driven my mother nearly crazy, with attempts to arrange, rehearse and dress amateur theatricals. During one bout, the back of the copper in the washhouse assumed the colours of the rainbow through the many packets of dye used in preparing these costumes. One attempt stands out from the many which I will recall. It was planned that the scene from Shakespeare's *Richard III* where Brackenbury has his interview with Clarence, just before he was murdered in the tower should be enacted. To fit up a younger sister with a coat of mail presented a problem. I tackled it in this way. Obtaining (I hope) honestly a vest and using silver paper backed with calico, I cut out dozens of scales, and patiently stitched them in overlapping rows to the vest. Having got so far, I felt a helmet was called for, so, using a basin as a mould, I used pasted brown paper and modelled a fairly presentable helmet. Then, to go on unto perfection, I found mother's blacklead brush used for polishing the kitchen range, and made the brown paper mache helmet look as though it had come from the Tower! BUT, alas, when my sister had struggled into this suit of mail, and it stretched to accommodate her shape, all the scales, being very light "stood on end like the quills of the fretful porcupine", while this, together with an unfortunate blacklead smudge on the cheek, sent the audience into fits of laughter, as the opening words were solemnly enunciated:

"O, I have passed a miserable night,
So full of horrid dreams and ugly sights" etc.

This however by no means daunted our spirits, and we came up again and again for more.

I have before indicated that while we were as a family "without God in the world", we were a happy family, kindly, generous, tolerant and rigidly honest. My father was quick tempered, so quick, that before he was half through some explosive utterance, he would be all apology. I remember some hard words being uttered between my two parents, but in the night he came where I was sleeping to assure me all was well, and that he was forgiven. I find that I too, cannot suffer fools gladly, and have to "count ten" when met by stupidity or obdurate opposition. Grace alone can cut through heredity.

It was quite a feature of home life to assemble in the parlour on a Sunday evening, while Dad read a chapter or two from one of Dickens' novels. Out of this in the year 1899, came into existence a manuscript Magazine called the *"The Home Circle"*. I have before me the bound volume, consisting of 642 hand written pages commencing September 1899 and concluding with June 1900. Apart from myself and an old school chum, no contributor, except my two parents, were above the age of fifteen years, some were less. The volume was fully indexed, and such topical entries as The death of Gladstone, The siege of Mafeking, A girl's protest against home work, Midsummer Night's Dream at Her Majesty's Theatre, Short stories, and a serial, A Poet's Corner, and ten articles on optics, give some of the range. Not one reference however can be found to Christ or the Scriptures. I cannot refrain from quoting the contribution made by my mother in the closing number. Her schooling had been practically nil. At the age of ten, she was already engaged in glove making, and in June 1900 our family consisted of father, myself and six sisters, so that my mother was hard pressed from morning to night to keep us all fed and clothed and clean.

"Dear Editor,
As it is the last Magazine this season, and I cannot write an article, I write to congratulate you on your undertaking, which I think has been a great success. I am exceedingly pleased with the work and it has brought out knowledge which otherwise would never have been shown. I am sure the contributors have all done their best"

Mother.

I must retrace a few steps because it is necessary to envisage something of the formative influence both the Bermondsey Settlement and later Toynbee Hall had on me. No spiritual benefit was either sought or found in these institutions, but He Who planned the goal, also superintended the fashioning of the earthen vessel. While my introduction to the Bermondsey Settlement was to acquire a knowledge of Greek, the Art classes and the Elocution and Dramatic classes soon captivated my attention, and all this be it remembered after many hours at a bench and a long walk home. The Art class was under the direction of Miss Beatrice Budgett, a Slade scholar and a relation of Dr. J. Scott Lidgett. From her kindly supervision I not only made progress in drawing, but became awakened to the gentler side of life. To this day I can remember, as she took the pencil from my hand, to correct an error in my attempt at drawing from the cast of the Lorenzo Monument, that I first saw a manicured hand - no varnish, no staining of the finger nails, but a revelation of what could be beyond the grime and the struggle of a Bermondsey environment. Miss Budgett not only devoted her time to come down to Bermondsey, but very graciously invited me to send her specimens of my drawing once a month for criticism.
One letter reads:

"I have shown your work to Professor Brown. He thinks that very probably it would be better for you not to attend a school of art - as in the Government Schools you may be obliged to do a great deal of unnecessary and mechanical work in order to pass examinations ... You would get on quicker if you worked alone and from time to time sent me your drawings and paintings to be criticised".

The interest that one and another took in the development of this Bermondsey boy, mitigated the otherwise frustrating pressure of circumstances and kept him sweet.

The
Bermondsey
Settlement

For all this care he looks back with amazement yet with gratitude. In the Elocution class I gained the prize for the paper on Theory, and played such parts as Shylock, Oberon and King Lear, fairly exacting for a youth of nineteen. Its value however was in the discipline of clear enunciation, appropriate gesture and the overcoming of "stage fright".

Retracing our steps once more, at the age of nine my finger was split open by a stroke of the cane I received, and for several weeks I enjoyed the privilege of excuse from all lessons and wandered about the school with my arm in a sling to the

evident envy of my school fellows. During this enforced idle-
ness I came upon the works of Shakespeare, and Macbeth in
particular, and was completely enthralled. In 1910 I walked
three miles from home to the Lyceum theatre, where I saw
Henry Irving and Ellen Terry play in Macbeth, and found myself almost word perfect. To this day the magic and mastery
of language that could produce the line
    "Unto the last syllable of recorded time"
still holds me in its grip.

A year or more after joining the Settlement, I was attracted to visit Toynbee Hall in Whitechapel, and there became a
member of the Art Student Club of which Alfred Parsons,
A. R. A. was President. Here I came under the influence of
Mr. and Mrs. Hancock Nunn, a Cambridge man and his wife
who devoted their lives to the betterment of folk like myself.
I must have responded to their kindness and was many times
invited to spend a day at their lovely home in Rosslyn Grove,
Hampstead. It was like being initiated into another world to
sit down to a snowy white linen table cloth, candle light, and
to be served by maids in caps and aprons. Again music had
a place as well as art, and I enjoyed singing such songs as
"Where the bee sucks", and discovering much hitherto un-
realized beauty. I should think that I owed more to these
kind friends than to any other up to the age of nineteen and
twenty. I should imagine I was what some would call "an
interesting kid".

Upon returning home one day from being out with some
fellow artists sketching, my father handed me a letter saying "I think you are the only one who can answer this".

                          Rosslyn Grove, Hampstead. N. W.
                                March 3rd, 1900.

Dear Mr. Welch,
        I am writing to you instead of speaking directly to your
son in order to save him from disappointment if you think my
proposal quite unpracticable.
        We have at Toynbee Hall a Travelling Club whose mem-
bers by travelling some 40 or 50 together obtain very much
reduced charges at hotels and fares by rail. This Easter
the Club, consisting of men and women students of Toynbee
Hall, is going to Venice and a few of the surrounding cities
of Italy, passing through Belgium, Germany and Switzerland.
        The Treasurer of the Club invites on behalf of his fellow
members one member of our Club to accompany them as
their guest.

After very carefully sounding several members of the Club and after much consideration, Mrs Nunn and I think that your son would be the most suitable member to accept the invitation. We suppose that he would be unable on his own account to afford the twelve guineas such an expedition would cost him, we gather that he is much less bound with regard to his holidays than almost any other member, and we feel sure from what we have known of him, that he would bring to such an expedition as much study as he possibly could give, so as to reap the fullest benefit from the new world of things into which he would be introduced. At the same time, he has shown so very much interest in Art and has made such rapid progress in his painting, that we feel he has earned the right to be considered first on such an opportunity as this.

Of course, a young fellow might jump at an offer like this without considering whether it would not unsettle him for his own work, and he might even risk his present situation for the sake of it, I want you to think this over with Mrs. Welch and let me know as soon as you can because if he is not to accept someone else may. If you think there is no harm in his going tell him by all means but if you think it wiser for him not to go, say nothing about it.

I am sorry Mrs. Nunn and I are not going with the party. It would have been an additional pleasure to have gone with your son. But several friends of ours will be going, and, as far as the expedition itself is concerned, I feel sure he will get nothing but the best influences from start to finish. Away about 18 days from April 11th.

With kind regards in which Mrs. Nunn joins me,

I remain,

Yours sincerely,

Thomas Hancock Nunn.

P. S. Going as the guest of the Club, your son could manage on a pound or so just for odd meals etc., for which the Club might not have contracted beforehand. If you care to see me about it, and care to call at Toynbee Hall between 7 and 8 on Monday, I shall be glad to see you. That or come up here to supper tomorrow evening at 8.30.

I approached the Oversight of the leather workers where I was employed for permission to take the three weeks off that the expedition entailed, but was met with the objection "such opportunities do no good to such as you, and your place will not be kept open if you take the time off". My immediate reaction was "I can get work at any time, but I shall never get an opportunity like this again". When I returned, my place was still open, all was forgotten, and when two years later I wished for time to go on a similar trip to Florence, this time paying my own expenses as a full member, the request was readily granted.

Jeweller's shops
Ponte Vecchio
Florence C·HW·59

I shall never forget the thrill of standing for the first time on foreign soil, reading foreign advertisements, and drinking in all the sights and sounds of such a venture. Our itinerary called for a stop at Lucerne, and Milan on the way out, and after staying for eleven days in Venice, stayed at Verona and Lugano on the homeward journey.

I asked myself "what can I do to show my gratitude?" and answered it myself by saying "I believe I shall say 'thank you' best, by enjoying every minute to the full", and so it seems did all concerned. As my birthday falls on April 25th I had my 20th birthday in Italy. I had naturally never set foot in a hotel in my life, and dinner of many courses had never come my way, but no foolish shyness or thrusting forwardness marred the happiness of a never to be forgotten experience. I read before leaving Ruskin's *Stones of Venice* and thrilled to stand on the little island of Torcello, and read over again the chapter dealing with the humble origin of Venice. Again, no spiritual blessing accompanied this further experience, nor were such in mind, but the gentle condescension of these gracious people fitted me all unconsciously for the otherwise intimidating experiences of a pioneer in spiritual things that were shortly to be mine. Looking ahead for a moment, the following letter, received from Dr. J. Scott Lidgett in the year the Vol. xii of the *Berean Expositor* was published, is of interest.

January 19th, 1922.

Dear Mr. Welch,
    Will you forgive a dictated letter. I have been trying to

write with my own hand, but the pressure of work is such that I find it impossible to do so within any reasonable time.

I cannot tell you how great was the thankfulness and pleasure your letter gave me. To have such testimony borne to the help the Settlement gave you in your early years is indeed a source of satisfaction and comfort to me. To render such help has ever been my hope, even in regard to those portions of our work here which may seem to be most secular.

Moreover, all my practical work here has sprung naturally out of the theology I have tried to set forth in my books.

I am so glad to hear of what you have been doing and are doing. May you be enabled to carry on and be made an instrument of growing good to all those who come under the influence of your publications! I will do my best to let those you mention know what you tell me about the help they gave you. The lady who taught you Greek was, I believe, Miss Lomas. She died more than thirteen years ago. Miss Budgett is a cousin of mine, and I will tell her. Mr. Jones ceased to be connected with the Settlement before the war, and I have not been in touch with him for more than three years.

I am still keeping on, though my colleagues have for the most part passed out of reach, and the death of my son, who was my mainstay and who was killed in the war has left me very lonely. Forgive this very imperfect letter, which is a most inadequate expression of my most grateful thanks to you for so kindly writing to me and for what you say.

With all best wishes,

Believe me,

Yours very sincerely,

J. Scott Lidgett.

Warden,
Bermondsey Settlement,
Farncombe Street,
Jamaica Road, S. E. 16.

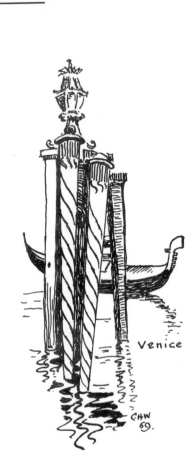

Venice

CHW
69.

The following attempt to put into verse, something of the feelings aroused by the first acquaintance with Venice was originally written for the Home Magazine, already spoken of.

Mrs Hancock Nunn commenting on this effort, said "every one who visits Venice under thirty, wants to write a poem". The reference to "love and peace and eternity" was not because I had at the age of twenty either hope or knowledge of salvation, but these sentiments were included as a poetic conclusion and to give an artistic finish.

VENICE THE FAIR

Beauteous still art thou in thy decay,
Thy beauty yet, outshineth living states,
It seemeth, thou art destined by the fates
                to be for aye.

Thy streets of glinting green, thy paths of sea
That mirror skies that crown thy glorious head
Of mid-day blue, or even's gold and red
                but jewels for thee.

Yet not as ropes of pearl on beauty's breast
That heave and sink with every living breath
But still and cold, like jewels bedecking death
        or marble crest.

The heart that once within thee swelled with pride,
At conquering galleys, or victorious arms,
Responds no more to triumphs or alarms,
        or wash of tide.

Thou lion of gold, who from thy field of blue
Look'st down but on this motley jostling throng,
Where are thy loyal sons, with freedom's song
        and heart so true.

No more with music, and with solemn rite
The wondrous sea, and Venice plight their troth,
And bind themselves to each, with solemn oath
        to rule with might.

So what see we? A picture of the past
A lovely picture, but a picture still
Of eyes undimmed, a heart that knows no thrill
        Nor e'er downcast.

And so with all thy beauty, thou dost lack
That touch of life, without which all must fail
To shine, and which our tears do not avail
        Or yet bring back.

Thy life sweet isle is gone, and soon shall we
Share in thy fate, and trouble too shall cease,
When we shall find the land of love and peace
        Eternity.

The reader will have gathered by now that much as I would have revelled in an opportunity to have had a college education, such under an all-wise Providence was denied me. At the same time I wish to leave on record my deep indebtedness

Trinity Cambridge

to a Cambridge man, Mr. Thomas Hancock Nunn, whose kindly interest has already been mentioned in these pages; and although the connexion with Cambridge itself may be tenuous the accompanying sketch of a well known feature of the University buildings may be permitted.

Through the mediation of Mr. Nunn, Oxford also had a share in opening my eyes to higher things, as I was invited to spend a long week-end with an Oxford don, and realized the great gulf that seemed to be fixed between all that had gone to make up my own life and the outlook and prospects of those more favoured. I was impressed with the venerable aspect of the Bodlian Library, little dreaming then that in later years the Bodlian would be sending a request that all my books should be placed upon its shelves.

The sketch of Magdalen like the one of Cambridge is inserted to be a reminder of these early kindnesses. One strange experience that I remember vividly was lunch on the top of

Magdalen. Oxford

Magdalen tower.

It has been my lot to discover that my writings have led some readers to conjure up a vision of "an elderly, scholarly, venerable, gentleman", to quote one reader, and in order that there shall be no doubt but that the earthen vessel whose fashioning has occupied us in this record, should be seen as a very homely ordinary unpretentious fellow, we will make our next entry one that is anything but high-brow.

The first example is a copy of a post-card sent home, and will give some indication of the relationship established between father and daughter, and the method adopted to stimulate enquiry.

"Dear Ruth,

Why would Droitwich be the place for you when you are a "pickle"? See the encyclopaedia. Please tell Mummy I hope to write this afternoon.

My love to *four* sweethearts now.

Dad".

The other is a post-card in lighter vein from Elroy Robinson announcing the birth of their little son, and my reply in kind, which did not in the least lessen our intense concern for the truth entrusted to us both.

"Here on the farm we've been getting lots of new things lately:

Fifty fuzzy white baby chickens,
Five little kittens as cute as the dickens,
Then four baby robins in a nest on the wall,
'N twice nine hungry piggys that sure can squall.

But these things above are just incidental
And not what we really want to tell you at all,
For the best and biggest and cutest addition
Who with his mother is in perfect condition   is:

DAVID JOHN: announcing "I arrived 2:20 p. m. May 6th. I weigh 9 lbs $6\frac{3}{4}$ ozs. and stand 22" tall. I don't want a thing except for you to know I'm here and that my Dad and Mom are

Elroy and Dorothy".

To this poetic effusion we replied in kind, as follows:

How nice to arrive	
Where the kittens are five	5
And fuzzy white chickens are fifty	50
It must seem very fine	
When the pigs are twice nine	18
And the four baby robins are nifty	4
You seem very tall	
And you cannot be small	
In fact you appear to be weighty	
So we send you our love	2 p. m.
And we hope we now prove	1
That the total now adds up to eighty	80

From Mr. and Mrs. Chas. H. Welch.

I loved your reply
Such adroitness in rhymes
Your versatile mind
In poetical lines!

Pray tell me what muse
   has you cold on the floor
For it seems you have talent
   and talents in store.   *Elroy*

"We have this treasure in earthen vessels that the excel-
lency of the power may be of God, and not of us"
                                   (2 Cor. 4:7).

WHEN IT PLEASED GOD ... TO REVEAL HIS SON

The time was now approaching when the spiritual crisis
took place for which all this previous preparation was permitted - a veritable Road to

Book Sellers Row
and
St Clement Danes
"Oranges and Lemons"
C·H·W/89.

Damascus. It was while I
was seeking a special gram-
mar in Bookseller's Row,
Strand (now entirely vanish-
ed) that a bill was put into
my hand by a young man
bearing some such notice as
the following:

SCEPTICS and the BIBLE

An address will be given on
   the above subject by:
Dr. L. W. Munhall, M. A. ,
                D. D.   U. S. A.
at Exeter Hall, Strand.

It must be admitted that
the word "sceptics" and not
the word "Bible" drew me
to that meeting in November
in the year 1900 and it was
with amazement that I list-
ened to a man who was most
evidently sane and scholarly, actually maintaining

that the Scriptures were true! As further meetings were

announced, I enquired of Dr. Munhall as we were leaving, what his subject would be on the succeeding evening. "We'll have the good old Gospel" was his reply. Now it may scarcely seem possible, but I did not at that time really know what the "Gospel" meant, and all next day I hesitated. "What's the use of wasting time?" "Perhaps it would be fair to let him speak for himself!" By the overruling mercy of the God Who at that time was unknown and unloved, I went to that meeting where "the good old Gospel" was preached. The text was taken from the Gospel of John "He that believeth on the Son hath everlasting life", and I passed from death unto life upon believing that simple testimony. I had no "views" on any doctrine of the Scriptures. Such terms as "Atonement", "Justification", "Reconciliation" and the like, were as the words of a foreign tongue. I had no concern as to whether John's Gospel was or was not for the present period, all I know is that it was blessed to my eternal salvation. This was my "Road to Damascus", as sudden and as complete as was the conversion of Saul of Tarsus.

At the close of the Gospel address Dr. Munhall quoted Romans 10:9 and called upon any who "believed" with the heart, to follow it by making a "confession" with the mouth. With great trepidation I responded and acknowledged the Saviour, As I stood there, feeling none too comfortable, Dr. Munhall gave a final word:

"This is not a matter of 'feeling'. There may be occasions subsequently when you will not 'feel' safe or saved, but this is a finished transaction based upon a finished work".

Thus started a new life, a new prospect, and a new goal. Upon reaching home after hearing the opening lecture on "Sceptics and the Bible" I had rehearsed the address with my father. Now as I journeyed home I realized I had something fuller and perhaps more decisive to discuss, and it would have been true of myself as it had been of the Apostle, that observing angels could have said for the first time "Behold he prayeth". Once again the message was repeated to my father, with the added personal comment "I believed and I have life". I needed no persuasion to make me attend the third meeting of this series. I was only too conscious of my abysmal ignorance of the very elements of revealed Truth. Again the preacher made known in simple terms the way of salvation, and again he quoted Romans 10:9 and made his appeal. I was naturally interested to see who would respond as I had done the evening before, and to my amazement and joy I looked round to see my father, with a face white with emotion, standing to acknowledge the same Saviour and Lord.

Here was a first-fruits indeed! And here commenced a faith of lovely simplicity that lasted until my father's death in his ninetieth year. My dear mother, and in course of time the younger members of the family, were brought by various ways or different instruments to a saving knowledge of Christ. Light had dawned in that Bermondsey home, and soon the consciousness of calling and commission was to make its urgent voice heard. For the moment let us pause, and gratefully acknowledge the wondrous grace that could save and enlighten those who were so darkened and dead.

GRACE AND GRACIOUSNESS at a TIME of CRISIS.

The fact that "straightway" after his conversion the Apostle could preach in the synagogue that Jesus is the Son of God (Acts 9:20 R. V.) or, as verse 22 adds, "proving that this is the very Christ", shows that before conversion his knowledge of the law and the prophets accorded with his zeal. True, as a Pharisee, he had imbibed the tradition of the Elders which stultified much of the Scriptures, a veil which could only be removed by an act of grace - yet it is evident that at his conversion Paul was already well stored with Biblical knowledge. In the case of the present writer it was not so. After conversion a most lamentable lack of the raw material and of Christian growth and witness was evident. Till nearly twenty one years of age the Bible had been a closed book. Those responsible for the Gospel campaign that had resulted in my conversion very wisely followed these Gospel meetings with a series of expository lectures given by that able Bible Teacher, Dr. W. H. Griffith Thomas.

The first of these studies was in the Gospel of John and I became acquainted - for the first time - both with the facts of the Gospel and with an excellent method of presenting the truth. Although it is forty-eight years since these lectures were given I can remember, as vividly as the night I first heard Griffith Thomas speak, how he introduced the teaching of John's Gospel. He said John's method seemed to be a truth made known, which was followed by a division among the hearers. This he made visible by the outline -

REVELATION   RECEPTION   REJECTION
(John 1:6-12).

Nothing could be simpler, though in many ways such an outline left much truth untouched, yet it came upon my susceptible and opening mind with freshness and force - a good omen of richer and fuller analytical studies that were yet to

be made. The four printed sheets giving the analytical outline of these studies in John's Gospel are before me as I
write, forty-eight years after they were delivered and are
treasured still. Next to my conversion they mark the most
decisive step in my early Christian experience.

Anticipating the story of the *Berean Expositor* a little, we
refer the reader to Vol. ii-iii (1926), p. 113 - where correspondence will be found under the initials W. H. G. T. On several occasions W. H. Griffith Thomas submitted questions, and
published the answers given in the *Berean Expositor* in his
own publications. I felt that it was nothing less than his due
that W. H. G. T. should know that the Editor of the *Berean
Expositor,* whose replies he was treating with such respect,
owed something to the lectures that he gave immediately after the Gospel campaign at Exeter Hall. We reproduce his
letter in reply.

Telephone   26 Park Road,
North 4841.   Toronto.
                                          January 3rd 1913

      "Dear Sir,
         Thank you for yours of December 16. I hope
the Editor of the *Morning Star* will insert something
from you in reply to the passage in question. It is
exceedingly interesting to me to have your testimony to those Exeter Hall Bible Readings in 1900. To
God be all the praise. I always read with great interest your various contributions to *Things to Come*
and the *Berean Expositor* and I also have your book
'Dispensational Truth'. I am unable to follow you
fully, but I have great sympathy with much that you
bring forward.
                  Yours faithfully,
                  W. H. Griffith Thomas".

This is one of five letters received from this fine student of
the Word. We will not reproduce them here, but give one or
two excerpts that will show with what intelligent and sympathetic interest W. H. G. T. read the articles in the *Berean
Expositor.*
Letter dated December 2, 1915, from 72, Spadina Road,
                                              Toronto.

      "Thank you very much for yours of Nov. 5 and enclo-
sures. I read all your articles with great interest,
and I am particularly partial to anything in the way

of Bible Structures, having learnt to look for those
from our good friend Dr. Bullinger. I shall be glad,
if you will send me from time to time, anything that
you issue which does not appear in the *Berean Expositor* and I will at once remit any cost on hearing from
you about it".

Letter dated May 10. 1917, from 42 St. George St. , Toronto.
"Just a line to say that I hope you are going to give us
a thorough treatment of Phil. 3:11, especially the ap-
parent hypothesis, 'If by any means I might attain'.
I am frequently asked questions on this text, and although I have looked pretty carefully to what our beloved old friend Dr. Bullinger has said in *Things to
Come* I cannot say I have yet been able to find an interpretation which meets satisfactorily, the thought,
which, to many minds, is suggested by the text ...
Perhaps, however, all this has been dealt with in
your promised article in the May number ..."

Letter dated May 29. 1917, from 42 St. George St. , Toronto.

"I wish you would in some way or other, justify your
view of Acts 1:25 stated on p. 76 of your May number.
I cannot find it supported by any commentator, and so
far as I can see, the twofold use of 'place' makes the
reference of the second far more natural to Judas
than Matthias. Your interpretation of the passage as
a whole is quite strong and convincing enough without this. There was a time when I was among those
who thought that Peter had made a mistake, but I
have long been convinced of the general line of your
article ... Let me also add that your suggestion on
p. 78 about John 6:29 is most interesting ..."

Here was a scholar, late Principal of Wycliffe College,
Oxford, and Principal of a Bible College in Toronto, not only
reading the *Berean Expositor* as one magazine among many,
but reading it with intense interest and manifesting that interest by continual correspondence. It is surely an evidence
of great grace that, knowing the history of the Editor as he
did, Griffith Thomas continued to read with interest the articles and books that came from his pen. It was equally an evidence of great grace that one with so few qualifications should
have been thus called and equipped. But this story of the
Berean Expositor is one of all-sufficient overwhelming and
sovereign grace from the beginning, and this testimony is
but an echo of the Apostle's words:

"By the grace of God I am what I am: and His grace which

was bestowed upon me, was not in vain" (1 Cor. 15:10).

At the south end of Drummond Road, the sky line was fretted by the two distinctive towers of Peek Frean's Biscuit Works.

Peek Freans Towers.

The drawing made in January 1959 shows the towers rather dwarfed by the adjoining modern extension, but all through my boyhood the sight of Peek Frean's Towers, meant "nearly home". My interest however goes much deeper than the biscuits for which this firm is famous; one of the shareholders, by name Huntington Stone, was used to direct my steps away from a ritualistic snare, into the paths of Biblical research. It came about in this way, Just converted, with practically no knowledge of the Bible, and no background to fall back upon, I became alarmed when I was told that at Baptism one became regenerate and a child of God. My father, although an avowed disbeliever at the time had me "christened" for he said, he had seen men lose the chance of a good job who had not been so initiated. I realized enough of the truth to know that no sprinkling of water on my infant brow had made me "a child of God" and the awful ungodliness of the pair that had stood as my god-father and god-mother reduced the whole to a blasphemous mockery. So I was about to go to an interview with a black-robed priest at the Clair College Mission, who might have turned me into a high ritualist, when a friend named "Wise" happened to say "You would enjoy the Bible Studies conducted by Huntington Stone at the house attached to Peek Frean's." Blessed be God, I responded, and learned at these gatherings what Bible study could mean. Five years later, I received the following letter sent by Huntington Stone to Mr Sutton, which may prove of interest:

Postal Address: Huntington Stone, Greenwich, S. E.

26th January 1915.

Dear Mr Sutton,

It was, I think, about a fortnight ago that I received

a copy of Mr. Charles H. Welch's booklet entitled "The Dispensational Place of the Lord's Supper", obtainable from Mr. Fred P. Brininger, 4 Spratt Hall Road, Snaresbrook, N. E. , and one or two leaflets, together with a note from yourself, asking me to study what you enclosed.

The study has proved interesting, and the Author evidently handles the subject very thoughtfully, and writes with a goodly measure of grace toward those who disagree with his interpretation.

The consideration of the theme has, I believe, proved profitable to me, though it is perhaps right to add that I have not been convinced that the arguments prove that the definite command to the Corinthian saints and "to all that in every place call upon the Name of Jesus Christ our Lord", bidding them to partake of the Lord's Supper "till He come" was withdrawn at the end of the last chapter of the Acts. At any rate, one does not find the instructions countermanded in any of the so-called mystery epistles. It is evidently true that when the time came for doing away with Old Testament rites, the Lord might have elected either:-

1. To substitute much more numerous new rites: or
2. To dispense with all rites between Paul's arrival at Rome and His return: or
3. To leave us with two very simple little rites, symbolizing and memorializing some very deep truth, and intended to be perpetuated until we see Himself.

This last alternative is what He has actually done, according to my understanding of the Scriptures.

Yours truly,

Huntington Stone.

About this time I was invited to help with a Ragged School Sunday School held in Marigold Street on Sunday evenings. There were about three hundred scholars, exceedingly poor and ill-clad, in addition there was a Gospel meeting attended by a number of poor old souls from the neighbourhood. While this work was of itself worth while, although somewhat arduous and very trying, something happened as a result of rendering this service that not only altered my whole outlook, but provided me with a loyal and loving partner for life. My sister, aged four years younger than myself had on a number of occasions invited a fellow student home, a lady by the name of Winifred. I had a suspicion that a friend of mine, named Will was attracted very much toward her, and hoping to expedite young love's dream, at Christmas time I sent him a

card bearing the device "Go in and WIN", playing on the lady's
name. This attempt however had repercussions. I found myself thinking "why should I not go in and win, instead?" When
I discovered that my friend Will was falling in love with my
sister (whom he subsequently married) I sent another card,
this time addressed to "Winnifred", and gave myself away,
when asked "how do you spell Winifred?" We met several times
in company with others, and then I suggested that on one particular evening we should meet "at the park gates" so that we
could go for a walk and have a talk. Alas, we had not stipulated WHICH gate, so that one of us waited with some suspense
at one end of the Park, and the other waited in vain at the other
end. I had a translation of Amos 3:3 very strongly impressed
on my mind, which reads: "Can two walk together except they
have MET?" However, we survived, and when I told my father
of our attachment, his heartening reply to me was "Boy, you
couldn't have chosen one we like better". From then on commenced a fellowship that has suffered, shared, rejoiced and
encouraged for over fifty years. Circumstances, which arose,
first by my association with the Bible Training College, and
then with the ostracism that followed the issue of *The Berean
Expositor* both of which services being carried on under great
financial strain, meant that we were engaged for twelve years
before our marriage could be arranged. This took place on
July 30th 1914, and war broke out on August the fourth!

Immediately following my conversion, my father and I, being quite ignorant of denominational differences, began to visit
various places of worship, and eventually made our spiritual
home at the Rotherhithe Free Church. After sitting under the
Evangelical ministry of Thos. Richardson for some time, I
with a few others felt impelled to be baptized, and this ordin-
ance was administered at Charrington Hall, in East London.

After a little interval I was invited to give a series of Bible
studies at the Drummond Road Baptist Chapel, which is immediately opposite Peek Frean's Factory, shown in a sketch
on page58. This series was among my earliest ministry.
At that time, in the vestry of the chapel one could be conscious of a battle of smells, the aroma of Colonial biscuits
meeting the smell of mustard pickles arising from Dodman's
Pickle Factory just behind the chapel. That conflict at least
is over, for on the site of the pickle factory now stands a
church hall, which suggests that in spite of many adverse
movements in the neighbourhood the work thrives.

We now arrive at an important moment in this story, which
formed another turning point in the history of the earthen
vessel.

AT THE FEET OF GAMALIEL

A young man named Percy W. Heward spoke at the Christian Band meeting at the Rotherhithe Free Church. His know-

Drummond Rd
Baptist
Chapel

CHW
'59

ledge of the Scriptures seemed fairly full, and learning that he was conducting a series of Bible Studies in a room kindly lent by the Mildmay Mission to the Jews in Philpot Street E., I attended with great profit. Early in these studies Mr. Arthur Page gave a series on "The attributes of God", and Elijah Bendor Samuel shed much light on the Scriptures in a series entitled "Hebrew Word Studies". Nothing very exciting occurred however until the Rev. James Neil, M. A. came in October 1902 and gave a set of lectures on "Figurative language of the Bible". The terms used were almost like Double Dutch (to use a colloquial figure of speech) and many of the names of the figures that were explained, like Hendiadys,

Hypocatastasis, Metonymy I could not spell. However, when
the series finished, I together with most of the class sat for
an examination. I have my answers before me, as I write,
fifty six years later and read the questions and answers with
mingled feelings. To the surprise of all concerned, my papers were marked First Prize. A consultation was held.
The man who had been marked Second was an older brother,
and actively engaged in Gospel work. It was felt unwise that
a novice should go clean over the heads of all, many of whom
had been Christians for some years, and my papers reveal
the markings that were adjusted, so that I should be second
instead of first. All this was done to save me from pride,
but whether such action could be justified I am not at all certain. However, this examination and its unexpected result
put me into prominence, and I was asked to become the
Secretary of the work. As "no good thing could come out of
Nazareth" my address was broadened to S. E. on notices, so
avoiding the name "Bermondsey". I wondered at the time
how this conformed with the teaching of the Word, but conscious of my own ignorance accepted both the second place
and the work of the Secretary without question. The classes
began to expand, and soon a larger meeting place was found,
and we were accommodated in the Commercial Street Baptist
Chapel, immediately opposite Toynbee Hall, but completely
destroyed by air raid later. This work grew and the need
for helpers increased, until Mr. Heward asked me to consider
whether it appeared to be the Lord's will to give up my daily
occupation and become the full time Secretary of the Bible
Training College as the movement was then named.

HISTORICAL NOTE

The B. T. C. began quietly as the Young Men's Bible Study
and Training Association. In 1902 the College was organized,
but during 1903 the Lord granted slow progress till the Pros-
pectus of 1904 was issued announcing a Two Years' Certificate
Course and Thorough Tuition, and excising the words "Young
Men's", so as to provide for brethren and sisters in Christ
of all ages, abilities and circumstances. Then numerous
applications were received, and granted. During 1904 the
Free Training Classes proved helpful to many (average
attendance 45-50), and likewise the examinations. The following College Societies have been formed - Student Preacher's Association (Gospel Ministers supplied), Students' Prayer Union and Missionary Union. Everything is prepared for
the Bible Training Colportage Association, etc. Bible Schools
and Conferences have been hopefully held (may there be

"increase" in every way). Twelve manuscript magazines are, to use a College term, - "in working order" - the majority monthly. Able lecturers have co-operated with the Principal and the Hon. Sec. (especially Rev. E. B. Samuel and Mr. S. Bloxsidge - Hebrew and Greek experts). Greek Classes have been formed. Noonday meetings at the College Chapel and the Offices have been conducted (both parts of the experience of Matt. xviii:20). A word concerning the latter (68 Fleet St) - opened in June - peculiarly central - visitors are welcomed, particularly intending or semi-intending students. Further information will be given gladly. Brethren come from Eltham, Erith, Fulham, Ilford, Mitcham. Walthamstow, Willesden, etc. "Not unto us, O Lord, not unto us, but to Thy Name give glory, for Thy *mercy* and for Thy *truth's* sake".

THE COLLEGE CREED

Published in November 1903:-

Dei Gratia.

I believe that the Bible, as originally given, not merely contained some thoughts of God, but that it was the Word of God; that it reveals the ruin of man, who by nature receiveth not the things of the Spirit of God, and seeth no beauty in Christ that he should desire Him; that it reveals the substitutionary character of the work of the Lord Jesus, according to the gracious counsels of the Triune Jehovah; that it reveals present holiness and the glories of heaven as inseparable accompaniments of regeneration; that it reveals the Divine command to true, spiritual witness; with the promise of guidance and blessing; and that it reveals the everlasting punishment of all who obey not God. Receiving these truths, I am constrained to know the things freely given me of God, and to show myself approved unto Him, a workman that needeth not to be ashamed, rightly dividing the Word of Truth.

CERTIFICATES, DIPLOMAS, ETC.

The reward of true study is found in Phil. 3:10. All true service brings Jehovah glory, and His people blessing. No rival aim should be permitted, or can be permitted, without sin. And the writer would grieve if any B. T. C. students thought more of his approval than the Lord's "well done" in that day - the double interpretation of "thought more of" suggesting two related actions.

Howbeit, there is no harm in Certificates, which may prevent a lengthy explanation, encourage to "painful" study by a reminder of that which is past, and take the place of primitive "letters of commendation". The danger is lest they become unattainable, or valueless by reason of an examiner's flexibility. We desire to avoid these errors. Brethren who attend College Classes during two years, and pass examinations (monthly, and final) will receive a Certificate stating facts. A third year well spent in College study will qualify for the Diploma, which is in no sense a rival to American degrees. These awards will *not* be given to men who manifest lack of spirituality - if any such can long endure the College labours. They will testify a general knowledge and love to the Word, a special acquaintance with special passages, and an ability to explain the Truth to others. The Preacher's Diploma is necessarily confined to brethren. "But if I fail in one or two exams. ?" The B. T. C. will not excuse errors, nor will it demand entire re-entry. Another examination on the same subject must be successfully taken before the certificate be granted.

In thus looking to the future, we would remember and repeat the words "if the Lord will". Persecution may hinder our purposes, but work out His, and, in any case, may this B. T. C. be found faithful "unto the Lord".

VACATIONS

The College has none. Be not alarmed. Our aim is primitive Christianity, and the servant of God is never off duty, unless he be undutiful. Our brethren take their holidays from B. T. C. Classes when they will - provided eight absences be the maximum, and notice be given. One has wisely attended every Class during 1904, but his record is unique. In accord with our desire for Scripturalness, students on "holiday" continue some studies and buy up opportunities for witness, rather than worldly pleasure. If the Lord will, in 1905, College caravan testimony during vacation, and *other* village work will provide a helpful change. On Bank Holidays Optional Conferences are held.

*   *   *   *   *   *   *   *

As we are tracing the pathway which this earthen vessel followed it seems right to reproduce here, what is the earliest piece of writing of mine that was put into print. The date of publication May 1904.

Expository Extracts

Collected and Compiled from College Class Notes

By the Secretary (Charles H. Welch)

"Dear fellow believers in our Lord Jesus Christ, it has pleased the God of all Grace, to rule and over-rule the studies at the College, to teach us, by many parts of His Word, the reality and awfulness of *sin* I, therefore, desire to pass on to you a few thoughts to the end that you may have (1) a more heart-felt experience of the exceeding sinfulness of sin, (2), a higher estimate of the inestimable blood of Christ, (3) a deeper gratitude to God for His Sovereign Grace and Eternal Love. Turning to Romans 3:9, we behold the inspired charge against the whole world, "That they are all under sin", inspired, in two senses - (1) Paul wrote by the inspiration of the Spirit and his writings are included in the "Scriptures" (2 Pet. 3:16), (2) his argument is founded upon Scripture "as it hath been written" (Rom. 3:10). Man's condition is "under sin", and in consequence he manifests the sins of verses 10-18. Can we not, by blessed contrast, say that "under grace" is the cause of all subsequent graces?"

These notes extend to a column and a half, but this extract will be sufficient for our purpose. The reader will note that the first word of this first published writing is the word "EXPOSITORY"!

In the following July accommodation was found and offices opened in 68 Fleet Street, where Correspondent Courses were printed and marked and the routine work of the College and the publishing was carried out.

"We rejoice to bear witness to the Protestant and spiritual character of the undenominational work undertaken by the Bible Training College. We believe that it meets a need and helps to train 'able ministers of the new covenant', who are so much wanted in these 'perilous times'. We heartily wish its officers God's blessing, and will gladly co-operate with them whenever possible, and invite the loving 'fellowship' of other saints in this testimony - to the glory of our gracious Lord.

Frank H. White.
Archibald G. Brown.
Samuel H. Wilkinson.

F

College Hall,
340 Romford Road,
Forest Gate.

"The Lord *hath been* mindful of us, *He will* bless us".

Among important gatherings and conferences held during the month, we would mention the S. P. A. Meeting, when Rev. J. B. Barraclough advocated, from Acts 10:34-43, the preaching of Christ Crucified, Risen, Glorified (a lesson, which, we may, by grace, be enabled to ex-emplify); and the conference on "Church Government". One sentence in particular was greatly blessed to the writer - " *Life* not Light - the condition of church membership". At one service the words "Spared not" as found in 2 Pet. 2:4, 5; Rom. .11:21; 8:32, were used to direct the saints to behold "the goodness and the severity of God" - but, alas, the emphasis laid upon the all-sufficiency of the perfect work of our Redeemer as Substitute and Surety, aroused opposition from a "stranger". Bills have been widely circulated and posters displayed, and much prayer and preparation have been offered unto the Lord in view of the coming Tent Mission, and of the Judgment Seat of Christ. Your spiritual and bodily presence and fellowship invited!

Charles H. Welch.

At this point, I would like to reproduce the letter written by Thomas Hancock Nunn on Sept. 14th, 1903, relative to my conviction that spiritual and Scriptural things necessitated my giving up, among other earlier activities, membership of the Toynbee Art Students Club. This severe cutting off is generally necessary for a beginner, who would otherwise be swamped and sunk.

Rosslyn Grove, Hampstead, N. W.
Sept. 14th 1909.

Mr dear Welch,
        I think I quite understand the experience which has led you to think that the Club may stand in the way of other, divinely appointed work. You have already passed indeed, the age at which such experience is common and as you realize the seriousness of life and the deep personal claim of God upon your individual soul I can only add my own gratitude and earnest God speed.
        But I think you may be mistaken (I do not for one moment say you *are* mistaken) in supposing that the call must carry you out of the Club. I don't wish you to exercise the

least particle of your own will in the matter. You must, I know, surrender all. It is the only way out. But in throwing up old associations, company, work, you may be introducing your own will where you least suspect it.

If all to whom God revealed Himself were to throw up current engagements and habits (not recognized as sinful) the very sphere of duty (their nearest) might in every case be forfeited. I merely want to point out as one who really cares for you and who also cares for the highest the Club can be made to be, not to disregard what may be your influence in the Club. I think there are indications that it is increasing and Mrs Nunn and I have found it very helpful and more so in our last expedition. Your only duty, I grant, is wise passivity. By withdrawing yourself from certain lines of work you may be more active in directing your own course than you really intend.

You know how sorry I shall be personally if you drop out of my life. I hope that need not be, even if you still feel that you ought to leave the Club.

I shall tell the Committee, if you are not there, that you are thinking of resigning and then we can talk it over when we return.

I am sure of your singleness of aim - only want it to take the best direction. With kindest regards, I am,

Yours sincerely,

Thomas Hancock Nunn.

* * * * * * * *

These extracts which cover 1904-1906 will give a little idea of the nature of the work into which I had been introduced. There were many hardships, especially in the matter of daily living, but these were cheerfully endured by reason of the lessons that were learned.

Soon after I commenced to learn some of the elements of the Hebrew language I passed a house in a back street off Whitechapel Road, which exhibited a sign in Hebrew characters in the window. I felt that this was an opportunity to test how far I had progressed.

מאנגלינג דוינג הערע

EREH ENOD GNILGNAM

"Mangling done here"

At first I could not make sense of the string of letters I had
translated until it dawned on me that it was a notice in English
words written in Hebrew letters and announced to the world
at large

"MANGLING DONE HERE"

Whatever else may be said against me, no one can accuse me
of trying to run before I could walk!
Later I learned to quote in the open air, Gospel texts in Yid-
dish, and being unconsciously something of a mimic, I was
hooted down and called a "m'shomed" or a renegade Jew, and
once was effectually silenced by having a cod's head, out of
the gutter pressed down on my head.

On one occasion a Jew challenged my quotation from the
Scriptures, saying "that is in your Protestant Bible". I explained to the crowd that while I based all my teaching on the
original Scriptures I, being an Englishman, naturally spoke
English. I asked my questioner whether he had a Hebrew
Bible, he said he had at home and the crowd agreed to wait
for him to fetch it. When he returned I asked him to find
Daniel 9:26 and to read it from the Hebrew. What he read
sounded something like   "YICHORETH MESSIACH V'AIN LO"
"Messiah shall be cut off and have nothing". He closed the
book and said "I have never read that before". You see the
Rabbi discourages "All computation of the days of the Messiah",
and so such passages, like Isaiah fifty three, are never read.
For a moment that crowd stood silent.

Soon after the close of 1906 a change came over the nature
and objects of the work.

While the B. T. C. continued as originally planned, my
heart was in the work, and I valued the training that I also
received while helping others. I was responsible for the
Elementary Greek class, and hoped that I would not prove to
be such a good teacher, that my pupils would catch up with
myself, who was at the same time a member of the *Advanced*
Greek class. It was a joy to see about 70 students devoting
two hours on three evenings a week for most of the year, in
concentrated studies of the Scriptures. The attitude of those
responsible was Calvinistic, and at the beginning had much
in common with those called Strict Baptists. One of the side
issues of the training led us into the open-air, and commenced a gruelling witness among the Jews.

There were many things that puzzled and distressed me
however which, owing to my lack of knowledge I accepted at
their face value, but I could not shake off the feeling that
there was an artificial "holiness" whipped up by continual
urgings to self mortification, so that later one member ran-

sacked London to buy a shawl for the expected baby, that was
drab in colour, "white" was forbidden being heavenly. In spite
of the grounding which this movement gave me in the Funda-
mentals I feel it would not be far from fact to quote of myself,
that "after the most straitest sect of our religion I lived a
Pharisee". To take a holiday was tantamount to backsliding
from grace, and I had to endure a lecture for not wearing a
black hat while spending a few days among gorse and heather.
It was all good discipline I expect like nasty medicine can be,
but it ultimately led to the rupture that opened the way for a
fuller understanding of the teaching of the Word. I took the
attitude, that while I was officially associated with this work,
I would stand loyally by Mr. Heward *in public* but state my
reasons for regretting many things to him in private. On one
occasion I was shocked by the subtlety of his reasoning. In
the neighbourhood of the meeting place in Forest Gate a man
was dying of cancer, and Mr. Heward was asked to visit him
with the Gospel. His immediate reaction was to send for me,
and say (for the first and only time) that I was a kind of Pastor;
he was but superintending from a distance, so it would be my
privilege and responsibility etc. etc. "Water falling drop by
drop, hollows out a stone", and eventually an incident occurred that led to a crisis. A lady of the meeting had passed on
to one or two fellow members a few copies of *Things to Come* ,
edited by Dr. Bullinger. She was summoned to appear before
Mr. Heward, and as a punishment for her action, was excommunicated and not allowed to participate in the Lord's Supper.
Mr. F. P. Brininger appealed against this drastic action towards his sister-in-law, and he too was excommunicated! I
felt that being an official of the movement, I could not endorse
this action, especially as it was at the end of a long list of
similar impositions. I make no claim to superior spirituality
for what I did, any more than Paul justified his calling the high
priest "A whited wall" (Acts 23:3). Neither would he have
justified the "contention" that divided Barnabas and himself
(Acts 15:39), but it was overruled, it brought into prominence
Silas, a Roman citizen (Acts 16:37) and Timothy (Acts 16:1),
for all unbeknown to either himself or Barnabas, a door was
about to open in Europe and the break had to come.

So, all unknown to myself, a door of utterance was about
to open, freed from the fetters that had bound me for several
years, and liberty without license was about to be entered.

My act was suicidal, I knew that what I intended to do would
cancel all the hopes, nullify all the preparation that the College Training efforts had held before me. I had been away
from the leather craft too long to think of returning and taking
it up again, and a blank yawned at my feet. Nevertheless I

made the offer on the spot to Mr. Brininger that I would go to him the outcast, and hold Bible meetings in his own house forthwith. At the time I was responsible for a mission among the Jews in Aldgate, and walked each Sunday (for riding in any form of vehicle was forbidden) the whole length of road from Forest Gate to Aldgate (about four miles, in all weathers) take the meeting and walk back again. This was willingly undertaken, believing as I did at the time that Sunday was "The Lord's Day" and equivalent to the Sabbath. As a sample of the approach employed at that time and in that mission, I reprint a composition which was exposed to view for all who passed by.

"SAYING NONE OTHER THINGS THAN THOSE WHICH THE PROPHETS AND MOSES DID SAY SHOULD COME" (Acts 26:22).

* * * The Law * * *

"And God spake all these words", we read	Ex. 20:1
When He, The Law, to Israel gave;	
And in that Law, (would they but heed!),	
He tells of sacrifice to save:	Lev. 1-5
Oh Son of Israel! broken is that Law,	Ex. 32:19
And God demands perfection – without flaw.	Lev. 22:21

* * * The Holiness of God * * *

Isaiah, in the Temple, saw	Isa. 6:1.
Exalted, High. The King of Kings;	Isa. 6:2
Bright Seraphim with holy awe	
Did veil their faces with their wings;	
And. "Holy, Holy, Holy", Lord, their cry	Isa. 6:3
Whilst man cries out, "unclean, unclean am I"	Isa. 6:5

* * * *The sinfulness of Man* * * *

All men, by nature guilty stand,	*Psa. 14:1-3*
The curse on all is justly laid;	*see Rom. 3:9-26*
They give no heed to His command,	*Deut. 27:26*
The Holy Law is disobeyed;	*see Gal. 3:8-16*
All we,like sheep,have turned - gone our own way;	*Isa. 53:6*
Nor tears, nor prayers, nor works our debt can pay.	*see Rom. 4:1-25*

* * *The Law's claims* * *

Yet whilst the Law of God still stands;	
Its claim OR curse, must *needs be* met;	
And love such as the Law demands,	*Deut. 6:4,5.*
No mortal ever offered yet	*see Matt. 22:37*
Hence by the deeds of Law, no flesh can be -	*see Rom. 9:26*
Made Righteous, nor can *man,* from sin set free.	*Psa. 49:8*

My action over the excommunication of Mr Brininger, necessarily made the question of further ministry and fellowship a problem for us all. In order to save the work from collapse, I agreed to the humiliating condition that I continue for another six months, but although still responsible for the Aldgate Mission, for the rest of that period I took with me *a written paper* which I had to read without comment! And when I eventually left, no one was told the reason but most felt that I had fallen into some disgrace which was being very kindly hushed up for my sake.

The letter that we reproduce here is dated 23/1/59, and is inserted as a first hand unsolicited reflection which we believe is necessary in the interest of truth. It is purposely left unsigned, but the original is in our files:-

"Dear Mr. and Mrs. Welch,

Now to thank you for your letter of good wishes and the photographic memento. When Paul said in 1 Thess. 2:17".. to see your face with great desire", I doubt whether a "photograph" would have satisfied him, don't you?

It is just over twelve years since I became acquainted with you both and the testimony for which you have stood for over 50 years, and though it has meant and still means the loss of "fellowship" I still rejoice before God for having been privileged to see the face of Jesus Christ unveiled more fully than ever before by this ministry.

There is much that one could say, but speaking personally, it has always been a matter of first importance to me, since salvation, to become assured that what a *man* may say, is in fact what *God* says. The result has been a progression *out* of one position *into* a better one.

I believed in "verbal inspiration" before I met you, but your treatment of the Word in demonstrating by structure the *key words* in their *God* given settings, has given that catch-phrase (i. e. verbal inspiration), a truer meaning than ever in my estimation.

Again and again I have rejoiced in spirit to see the careful analysis of words and their correct application. "What is chaff to the wheat saith the Lord?" I am glad too that this method of teaching the Word is not exclusive, by which I mean, you are not afraid to compare and study the writings of other believers and wherever possible to make this evident in your conclusion.

Perhaps you would like to know what it was that, as far as I can remember, became a deciding factor with me in accepting that the "church" of the Acts is not in being today. As you know, it was part of Mr. Heward's belief that Peter and the rest of the apostles erred in their appreciation of the "mind of God" (a favourite phrase with him), hence "their mistakes" in practice. Hence the *very first* recorded question of the apostles is a *mistake*! Instead of being a *clue* an index to their state of *mind* induced by the *Lord's instruction* during 40 days when He opened the Scriptures *and* their *minds* to receive them!! How I rejoiced when, by you simply referring me to Luke 24:45 I was able to regard the apostles as being, *at least* as intelligent as I am, and not stupid clots. The Lord did indeed have to chide them for being foolish and slow to believe all that the prophets had spoken, but surely part of that stupidity consisted in the fact that they did not at that time perceive how restoration would come via Christ's death and resurrection, and not in their expectation of restoration.

Luke, at the beginning of his gospel in chap. 1:32, 33, 67-79 etc., and at the end in 24:21, shows that Restoration of the Kingdom dominated the mind and rightly so. Then another "mistake" was the choice by lot of Matthias! But again, you refer me to the Lord's words in John 15:27, and the Psalms which spoke of Judas, confirmed again by the Lord at Passover; all of which became just reasons for Peter's decision. I saw how feeble was the attempt to thrust Paul among the apostles for the sufficient reason that John 15:27 disqualified him. Added to which Paul's own testimony in 1 Cor. 15 disassociated himself from the twelve.

Did you know how P. W. H. argued out of that difficulty? He said that the Holy Spirit gives us a hint that Matthias was not really an apostle because wherever we read "the twelve" the word "apostles" is omitted, and where we read "the apostles" the word "twelve" is omitted!! This is clutching at straws with a vengeance.

Then further, reading your analysis of Peter's reactions to the vision of the sheet from heaven; his mode of speech conveying apology, surprise, hesitation in dealing with Cornelius and the other apostles, showed me that either we are dealing with a dull, unimaginative man, who continues to misuse his function as the holder of the keys of the Kingdom of the heavens, or one who is acting consistently with the testimony entrusted to him up to that point and thus speaks accordingly. Seeing this to be the only sane way to view Peter's response, made me realize that the familiar quotation of Acts 2:42 was out of place today, for these believers being instructed by the apostles now saw Jesus of Nazareth as their Messiah and their rightful King, and consorted together in the Temple with new found joy. The place is Jerusalem, the time is Pentecost, why should Gentiles be there? Had anything changed since Christ was crucified 50 days before?

Reverting to Acts 2:42 we read "they continued stedfastly in the apostle's doctrine". Now taking the viewpoint of some that these apostles had a mistaken attitude about their heavenly calling (they were not spiritually minded enough) why do they insist we should get back to the apostles teaching? Of course they make the common mistake of confusing later revelation with what has passed, reading the future into the present and so on. How should any one today know what the

apostles taught then if what they preached then is ignored?
I had heard too, different views about "the olive tree" of
Rom. 11; the usual one allowing that the believer can be lost.
A true appreciation of Israels priority during the Acts, Gen
tiles being added to provoke, if possible, a response from the
nation, it came as added cause for joy. Then too, I am grateful for the study relating to the "millennium", over against the
teaching that Christ will rule in the hearts of everyone on
earth for John 16:7-11 to become true, so that He will not need
to be on earth! Dan. 2 relating to the destruction of all kingdom typified in the image, in one blow, followed immediately
by Christ's reigning over all the earth, does not allow of men
bringing in universal righteousness and peace because ruled
by the Holy Spirit prior to that. Many other things of course
could be said, but that I be not further tedious unto thee,
speaking of ourselves our health could be better, things are
at pressure in every way, we feel our need of strength and
courage and want always to be grateful remembering that we
can be strengthened with all might, according to His Glorious
power, unto all patience and long-suffering with joyfulness.
Ours is a walk of faith, hence "patience" - long-suffering with
joyfulness is logical. The end is sure, intervening "curtains"
of trouble and difficulties make no real difference.

We are also glad of the tapes and so share in the spoken
ministry.

Both my wife and I send you both our love and best wishes
for the future.

signed (   )

THROUGH BONDAGE TO LIBERTY

When at the invitation of the Bible Training College I became the Secretary, as already mentioned I felt that I had
found a cause to which I could well devote my life and energies.
This however was not to be, but the discipline and the con-
tacts made were most certainly divinely ordained. Out of a
series of events that were of themselves the occasions of
much sorrow and heart searching, there emerged one out-
standing fellowship to which every reader of the *Berean
Expositor* must be for ever indebted. I refer to the loyal and
gracious partnership of Mr. F. P. Brininger, a fellowship that
lasted for forty years and which ceased only with his death
in November 1947.

It would be wearisome to recount the gradual change that
came over the work of the Bible Training College, and how
the idea of founding a "primitive church" took the place of the

"training college", which change bred a most censorious spirit.
This primitive church was to be founded on "the Sermon on the
Mount" and Acts 1 and 2, with an obligation to attend the Lord's
supper that was almost tyrannical in its insistence.

Side by side however with this undispensational attempt to
form a "primitive church" there had been a series of studies
in the epistle to the Ephesians, in which I took a prominent
part, and the growing conviction - that the present dispensation was not concerned with a church built on the lines of
the "Sermon on the Mount" or Acts 1 and 2 - suddenly blossom-
ed into full flower by an incident that marks a crisis in the
testimony to the truth for which *The Berean Expositor* stands.

In the early publications connected with the Bible Training
College, the writings of Dr. E. W. Bullinger were reviewed,
quoted and advertised, but as the "primitive church" idea pre-
vailed, Dr. Bullinger's name was dropped, and finally any mention of his works forbidden. I was definitely assured that Dr.
Bullinger was as bad as, if not worse than, a higher critic
because he "cut up" the Word of God! Since that time I have
been honoured by being designated "worse than Dr. Bullinger"!

Before we rehearse the events of 1908-9 which led to active
fellowship with Dr. Bullinger and the issue of *The Berean
Expositor*, a summary of what has already been reviewed may
be of service.

Nov. 1900	Converted at Exeter Hall under the ministry of Dr. L. W. Munhall.
Nov. 1900	Attended the first exposition of Scripture under Dr. W. H. Griffith Thomas.
Nov. 1903	Approximately at this time I began to attend meetings for Bible Study at Central Hall, Phil-pot Street, which although held in the premises of the Mildmay Mission to the Jews, was entire-ly independent of that Mission, the room being graciously lent for the work.
Early 1904	Sat for the examination held as a result of at-tending a course of lectures by the Rev. James Neil, M. A. , on "The figurative language of Scripture". To my own surprise, and to the surprise of all concerned my paper was origin-ally marked 1st prize, but by agreement, sub-sequently re-marked 2nd prize. This led to:
March 1904	The appointment as General Secretary to the Bible Training College. Here commenced an active period of Bible study and teaching, com-bined with an open-air testimony among the Jewish population in the vicinity of Petticoat

Lane, a training ground for Gospel and Bible speaker second to none.

April 1904 An appeal for financial help so that a full time Secretary, and an office and library could be provided appeared in the Monthly periodical.

May 1904 "We rejoice to say that some of the students have exemplified grace in that they have amplified their gifts, and consequently Mr. Welch is 'given wholly' to the College work". Extract from published announcement. In this month moreover there appeared for the first time the following:

S(ERMON P(OINTS
by   a
TUDENT   REACHER
Edited by Charles H. Welch

and whether it be suggestive of future ministry or without special significance, the first text under this heading, was Ephesians 2:13.

July 1904   68, Fleet Street, E. C. becomes the Central Office of the Bible Training College.

July 1905   College Hall opened for residential students and for Conferences, etc.

Dec. 1906   The Crisis. Fellowship commenced in the home of Mr. F. P. Brininger which ultimately led to the publishing of *The Berean Expositor,* and all subsequent witness.

Sept. 25, 1907 All connexion with the Bible Training College and its subsequent ecclesiastical developments, brought to an end.

Now commences a story of endurance and physical hardship that up till now has been known by but a few. Those days are happily so far back, and such wondrous grace has been so manifest along the upward though difficult path, that we can venture to speak of those days with some measure of detachment.

The letter which is printed below is of interest to all who are concerned with the Editor's fight for the truth "rightly divided". It is an unfinished rough draft of a letter sent to the leader of the movement in which I served as Secretary for several years. There are evidences of confused ideas that need clarifying but speaking generally, it will be seen that as early as 1908, the general lines of Dispensational Truth were perceived, and which were seen more clearly when complete freedom was attained. We have purposely omitted names and places, as no good would be done by their publication, and some would be unnecessarily hurtful. This letter was written when I was not quite twenty eight. I am now approaching my eightieth birthday and there is little I would alter, apart from phrase and style.

London, 1908.

Dear ......

I have been waiting for some weeks before writing to you, for I feel that this letter will contain that which will cause a greater separation between us or, (which I cannot believe) will revolutionize the work at ... It is not pleasant to the flesh to know that one is courting the censure of those whose regard in spiritual things has been valued. Nevertheless I trust I have learned in heart as well as in head that knowledge brings with it a painful yet blessed responsibility. After prayer and I must confess much hesitation I look for grace to write you, and realize that if you do not believe the content of this letter to be true, that you will have no alternative but to class me with those who go contrary to the Word of God*.

In the first case I must confess that I never felt easy over your attitude towards the teaching of the Scriptures concerning 'The Body', and now looking back I can see that the publication of your conclusions on this subject marked a turning point for me, for which you are partly responsible.

According to your view of the Word, Satan's great attack was against the manifestation of the One Body, in other words the assembly position as recorded in the Acts and 1 Corinthians. You have had the church on earth so much in your mind that the heavenly reality has become dim (pardon any appearance of rudeness I seek grace to exercise true meekness**) and you would in other points condemn the method of interpretation you have adopted in this:-

"Paul's conflict was related to the heavenlies, which cannot be interpreted of the assembly on earth. Satanic power was levelled against the saints who like Paul were constrained to leave Judaizing Christians, even though they were Apostles, and who boldly proclaimed the truth of the One Body and the heavenly calling." Here the article referred to assumes in my estimation its significant and awful position. Satan saw

* This is in fact what happened and was quoted against me as aptly fitting my case.

** The reader will perhaps sense that the stand taken as indicated by this letter cost the writer exercise of heart at the same time.

that we were beginning to appreciate these blessed truths. Ephesians was being studied and he must seek at all costs to prevent that long buried truth, the teaching that is summed up in the words "In the heavenlies in Christ" from being proclaimed - and so you suddenly framed the proposition 'A Body is something visible', logic then compelled you to continue 'No visible Body is on earth now, therefore the Body does not exist'. You faced the problem, came to the conclusion, brought the study of Ephesians to a close, and since then your teaching and exhortation has been based upon Acts 2, etc., the typical character of the books of Ezra and Nehemiah as applied to church conditions, and the special teaching for the present period has been allowed to fall into the background, the Apostle's great argument 'See what you are in Christ, and walk accordingly' has given place to precepts and commandments, a tendency to look within, and so Satan's object was attained. You have of late insisted upon Matthew 5-7; bear with me when I draw your attention to the fact that whereas Matthew 6 says 'forgive us, as we forgive' Ephesians says 'forgive because you are forgiven'. My own dear father has voiced something of this feeling. Walking to the meeting he said to me: 'I sometimes feel in the week with its worry and distress, that I yearn to hear something of what the Lord has done for me. I hear much of what I ought to do, but how empty it all seems.

2 Corinthians 3 says: 'Beholding the glory of the Lord we are transfigured' the Lord's people being in Christ, there is a new creature. Seeing things through other men's spectacles I have in times past used the epithets 'Jewish' or 'ultra-dispensational' when speaking of the work of others. Upon more careful study I feel that we can see Satan at work again. In the movement of 1840, the blessed truth of the standing and calling of the Church was re-discovered, and for a time J. N. D. and those with him saw the distinction and emphasized it, but made some unwise and far-fetched statements. B. W. N. saw the tendency and went to the other extreme and practically denied the peculiar element that characterizes the epistle of Paul*. What do we really find? Malachi is not the end of inspired Jewish history, neither is Matthew. Inspired Jewish history reaches to the last chapter of the Acts, there the nation of Israel is recognized as such, blessing is promised to them upon repentance, and Gentiles blessed through them. Romans 15 opened my eyes to this, and if we perceive the truth of Romans 15:8, why should we use the epithet 'ultra'

* These remarks refer to long discussions arising out of the teaching and divisions among the early brethren, and would have then been understood far more than it is possible for anyone now reading them to do.

of those who apply this teaching to the gospel that contains it? That gospel teaches that Christ came as the Messiah. His opening proclamation is concerning the kingdom. He gave its laws, and He was, as king, rejected. After His ascension the final testimony was given to Israel accompanied by signs and wonders. Every accompaniment of Pentecost was Millennial, the preaching was purposely addressed to Israel, and the promise was made of the return of the Lord upon their repentance. It seemed to me an ominous evidence of the power of one's own opinion which led you to give public utterance to the idea that Peter made a mistake in Acts 1 and 3. In Acts 3 Peter was but following out the principle expressed in the parable of the Nobleman who had gone into a far country to receive a kingdom and return. The final rejection of Israel and the use of Isaiah 6 in Acts 28 is crucial. * Before this Paul had written Corinthians, Galatians and Romans. Already he had suffered at the hands of those, who, though believing that Christ was the Messiah, were still zealous of the law (Gal. 2) and although you quote this chapter I fear you approximate to Peter and James rather than to Paul. Nevertheless, these leaders were compelled to allow Paul to preach his glorious teaching of 'in Christ' even though some said his teaching led to licence, yet he still emphasized their freedom in Christ.

If you will compare the epistle to the Ephesians with the epistles written before Acts 28 you will see a noteworthy difference. For example the Jew is personally addressed in Romans and occupies a considerable space in that epistle (chapters 2-4, 9-11). In chapter 11 it is definitely taught that Gentile blessing is through the Jew, and the associations, with the hope as set out in Romans 15 are Millennial. So in 1 Corinthians, the gifts were a witness to Israel, they are called in Hebrews the powers of the age to come.

Paul could only speak to spiritual ones at Corinth concerning the mystery (cf. milk and meat). Paul's 'sin' (as taught)** is overruled to take him to Rome and there Ephesians, Colossians and Philippians were written, each epistle refers to the fact that he was a prisoner - why? To show that Jerusalem was rejected at the centre ('beginning at Jerusalem'), and that Rome, the city of the Gentiles, with Paul the prisoner, taking its place. He can now declare that which it would not have been expedient to utter while Israel (humanly speaking) had the opportunity to repent. The dividing line which affects us is Acts 28.

* Acts 28 as the dispensational boundary is evidently seen.

** This was immature teaching given at the time concerning Paul and his journey up to Jerusalem, and is rectified later.

You will remember that we saw very blessedly, that we were
in a dispensation of foreshadowing 'the earnest', but we have
not seen this in true perspective. From Acts 2 to 28, gifts,
assemblies and the position of Israel - all were prophetic of,
and foreshadowing the Millennium. After Acts 28 it is the New
Creation, that is foreshadowed.

This new creation does not come in the epistle to the Hebrews, the object of Hebrews being very different. Hosea
three declared that Israel shall abide many days without a
King, Priest or Sacrifice, and Hebrews points to the only One
who sums up these offices in Himself.   In Hebrews is Paul's
final appeal to his brethren still entangled in Judaism. To me,
your exposition of Hebrews six places you on the wrong side
of Acts 28, and is consequently undispensational. Paul exhort-
ed the believer to 'leave' these things. You would make them
fundamental . . . . . . "
Here the rough draft ends, but the line of argument is clear
enough for our purpose.

As already mentioned I left the work of the Bible Training
College - to which, in its earlier form, I would have willingly devoted my whole life - and having done so a dreadful blank
faced me. Unemployment even in days when Government assistance is a regular and recognized thing is nevertheless
dispiriting, but in the year 1907 no organized assistance for
the unemployed person existed. I had been away from all con-
tact with daily business for long enough to make re-entry impossible. However, to pass to the spiritual history, meetings
now began to be held regularly at the home of Mr. Brininger
where a handful of believers met for the unfolding of the
Scriptures. One of the earliest subjects that came up for consideration was the doctrine known as "Conditional Immortality". The teaching which I had hitherto endorsed, held to the
orthodox view concerning the immortality of the soul, eternal
conscious torment of the lost, and the consciousness in an
intermediate state of those who had died. The very prospect
of reconsidering so formidable and solemn a set of doctrines
was rather intimidating, but at length the light dawned and
the Platonic doctrine that had been foisted upon the Scriptures
was perceived to be untrue, and the glorious Gospel of "Life
only in Christ" irradiated our new endeavours. This, wonderful as it was, was not the main quest before us. During the
transition days when the Bible Training College waned and
the idea of founding a Primitive Church was growing, the
unique character of the dispensation of the Mystery was making itself felt, but could neither be followed nor expressed.
With the shackles broken, the truth began to be perceived in

C. H. W. taken about
1937.

W. J. W. taken about
1937.

G

A Sketch of Dad

The house of Mr. and Mrs. Linden,
Rockford, Illinois.

Great Grandfather

Great Grandmother

A BEREAN

IN

AMERICA

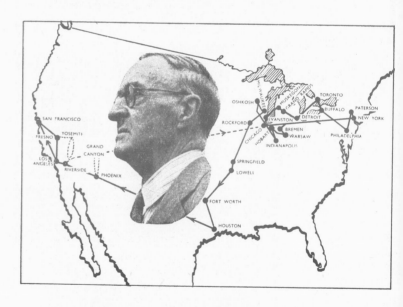

A brief record of the visit and reception of

CHARLES H. WELCH

EDITOR OF THE BEREAN EXPOSITOR

MAY AND JUNE 1955

Mother

F. P. Brininger
Charles H. Welch
W. G. Whitaker
on board the
Liner, about
to leave for
Canada.

Mother and Child
C. H. W. age 13 months

Brother and Sister,
C. H. W. age 6 years
Kit   age 2 years

something of its pristine glory.

Before me, as I write, I have a small note book which bears on its front page the legend "1d., 150 pages, ruled and perforated", and that penny note book contains the earliest indications of the way in which the truth was sought and discovered. On the first page are notes dealing with the Mysteries of Scripture and their connexion with Israel. On page two are found notes: "Inspired history ends at Acts 28". "Acts 28 the turning point. Before Acts 28 and after". These were the themes, with which this new quest for a truth opened.

On another page appears a structure, the first structure of which I have record, it is a combination of the various words "to make known" and "to enlighten" that occur in Ephesians and Colossians. Later in the notes is another entry of significant importance. It reads "Acts 28 and the epistles on either side". This, as I shall show presently was an epoch-making note so far as the witness of *The Berean Expositor* is concerned. Other notes that are suggestive are "Fulness - look up"; "Meaning of Dispensation".

In the same note book is also a set of notes which at first sight appear to have no connexion at all with this story. They are the names and addresses of Education Officers in different parts of the country, and among them at times appear references to "drawing" and "art". It will be necessary, if we are to appreciate the atmosphere and circumstances in which the ministry of the Mystery was entered and sustained that we turn aside for a moment from spiritual issues to consider the more mundane things of daily living.

When I gave up my daily business, I accepted a salary lower then that which I had previously earned, and after a few months, voluntarily relinquished all salary, and subsisted on gifts made from time to time by the Lord's people. I never actually wanted, but many a time came extremely near to it. It will readily be understood that when I left the work connected with the Bible Training College nine months after making my protest, my coffers were practically empty. Had it not been that I was welcomed back to the old home during this trying period, there may have been no sequel to this story. As it was I found moral and material support to make a venture.

I enquired at a Technical School concerning what qualifications were necessary for Art Teaching, and was told that I needed (1) The Art Class Teacher Certificate and (2) the Art Master Certificate. My heart sank when I learned that it was usual to take three years to gain the Art Class Teacher Certificate! I was then 27 years of age and contemplating a return to school! To cut a long story short, I passed all exam-

H

inations and submitted all necessary sheets of drawings except one in the first year, and won the King's Prize for design
in the second year. As a matter of interest and an evidence
that "faith" was not left uncombined with "works" we give a
list of the certificates during that trying period.

1908	First class	Drawing in Light and Shade.
	First class	Model Drawing.
	First class	Design stage one.
	First class	Geometrical Drawing.
	Second class	Drawing common objects from memory.
1909	First class	Architecture.
	First class	Memory Drawing of Plant Form.
	First class	Stage 2 Modelling Design.
	First class	Perspective.
1910	First class	Stage 2 Design. (This received the King's Prize).
	First class	Modelling the Head from life.
	First class	Painting Ornament.
	First class	Principle of Ornament.
1911	First class	Anatomy.
1912	First class	Painting from Still Life.
	Second class	Drawing from the Antique.

In addition to these examinations, sheets of drawings 22"x
32", comprising Geometrical Examples, Elements of Design,
Plant Form, Shaded Models, Orders of Architecture, Perspective, Applied Design, Antique Form, Shaded Ornament,
Historic Ornament, were all submitted and accepted.

Any who have made copies of testimonials, and who have
known the sinking of heart as the fruitless repetition drives
the iron into one's soul, may read with sympathy the following:-

London County Council
Camberwell School of
Arts and Crafts, Peckham Road, S. E.
23rd January, 1912.

Sir,
I have much pleasure in testifying on behalf of Mr. Chas. H.
Welch as assistant master.
Mr. Welch is a sincere hard worker bringing to his work
mental qualities of high order and an outlook upon the world
of teaching which, whilst recognising the good on traditional
methods, would infuse ideas in forms of drawing that would
make his work inspiring.
Mr. Welch is a lucid, methodical lecturer and freely uses

the blackboard in demonstrating: his own practice is of a very good type both in design and draughtsmanship and I am confident that the sincerity, earnestness, and zeal he has always shown would soon be reflected in the work of his pupils.

I am, Sir,
Your obedient Servant,
(Signed) W. B. Dalton,
Principal.

The Second testimonial:-

London County Council.
Orange St. Evening School
(M. & F. Dept).
W. Southwark LCC Electoral Area.
March 1st, 1912.

I have pleasure in saying that
Mr. Chas. H. Welch
has worked as Drawing Master, for the last 3 years in these Evening Classes. In spite of the difficulties arising from the facts, that the pupils are drawn from very poor homes, and that the classes are quite free, the interest of the scholars has been aroused, and sustained earnest work has been accomplished, and good results have been secured.

Mr. Welch has an excellent influence over his class, and I am pleased to see that he has the power to awaken some artistic instinct in the most unlikely pupils, whilst the clever student is really very fortunate to be under his excellent tuition. He gives much forethought to the preparation of his lessons and they are systematically arranged on a thoroughly educational basis. He is a very hard and conscientious worker sparing neither time nor trouble for the good of his class.

I consider this specially difficult school, a most severe test of an Instructor's discipline and teaching power, and Mr. Welch has, in my opinion, proved himself, even under these conditions, to be a teacher with exceptional ability.

(Signed) George E. Brown,
Responsible Master.

This second testimonial covers the period when I practically "lived" on the earnings that accrued from this very testing centre of activity, which were so low, that to state it would probably sound as uttering an untruth - we leave it at that, realizing that "Out of them all the Lord delivered me", "that the preaching might be fully known".

I commenced teaching in the L. C. C. Evening Schools at the lowest rate of pay, and in the second year my entire earnings from this source averaged 10/- per week! And while this struggle was going on, and with such exceeding limitations to contend with, *The Berean Expositor* was published. Truly, if in nothing else, I could quote the Apostle's words with some measure of feeling-

"As poor, yet making many rich" (2 Cor. 6:10).

Toward the end of 1908 I felt moved to write to Dr. Bullinger. I had seen a copy of *Things to Come* while still acting as Secretary to the Bible Training College, and although I had been warned against the Doctor's "heretical" teaching, much that I read struck a familiar chord. After an interval I again saw an issue of *Things to Come* and was amazed to see an article which I could have duplicated from my own notes. Evidently, I thought, whoever wrote that article had moved along similar lines to myself, and so, with some trepidation I plucked up courage to write to the Doctor, asking him for an opportunity to see him and talk over one or two important points in which I felt bound to differ from his findings.

One of the points raised in this letter reads:

"Are we not liable to be using transitional things if we do not discriminate in epistles like Corinthians and Romans - truth tempered to suit the time when the Jew was a factor to be reckoned with, but not so now".

After some delay, the Doctor granted me an interview at the offices of the Trinitarian Bible Society, Bury Street, London., and that hour's interview proved to be the most critical turning point in my life and ministry. The Doctor invited me to say what was troubling me, and I feared, that after all, he would smile indulgently, pat me on the shoulder and tell me to go home and forget all about it. Again I plucked up courage and here is a transcript of our conversation.

Myself - From your writings Doctor, I believe I am right in saying that you do not believe "The Church" began at Pentecost, but rather, that the Dispensational Boundary must be drawn at Acts 28?

Dr. Bullinger - That is so. I have made that quite clear.

Myself - Well, what seems to me to stultify the position you have taken regarding Acts 28, is, that you nevertheless treat the whole of Paul's epistles as one group, starting with Romans, ending with Thessalonians, with Ephesians somewhere in the centre.

To my amazement and joy, the Doctor looked at me for a moment, then slapping his thigh with his hand said:

"That scraps half the books I have written. But we want the Truth, and the Truth is there in what you have said".

I felt that here was indeed "grace". Dr. Bullinger was a man of world repute, a scholar and an elder. I was a young man of 28 years and unknown. We spent the remainder of our brief interview in considering the dispensational implications that arise from observing the relation of Paul's epistles to the boundary line of Acts 28 thus:

Acts 28.

Epistles Before.		Epistles After.
1) Galatians	1)	Ephesians
2) 1 Thessalonians	2)	Philippians
3) 2 Thessalonians	3)	Colossians
4) Hebrews	4)	Philemon
5) 1 Corinthians	5)	1 Timothy
6) 2 Corinthians	6)	Titus
7) Romans	7)	2 Timothy

At the close of this most important interview, Dr. Bullinger said:

"I will now let you into a secret. I am just commencing what I feel sure will be my last work *The Companion Bible.* I have prayed that someone be sent along to relieve me of some of the pages in *Things to Come.* You're the man".

At first I demurred. I felt that the standard set by the articles in *Things to Come* was above my attainment, and I was also rather intimidated as I visualized the calibre of its readers. At the time when I was to all intents a pagan, many of the readers of *Things to Come* were advanced Christians. However the Doctor persuaded me that the call was of the Lord, and so in March 1909 there appeared an article entitled "The Unity of the Spirit (Eph. 4:3). What is it?" One passage in the article reads:

"All other scripture that had ever been written, had been written in connection with Israel. The epistle opens up the 'Mystery hidden away from the ages', the One Body, the One New Man - the subject of enquiry".

This was written as an immediate response to the Doctor's invitation, but I felt that to be effective much spade work was called for and so, in April, there commenced a series entitled *"Dispensational Expositions"* which continued until the magazine came to an end. In the February of the same year (1909), *The Berean Expositor* was first published, and any who possess the original issue, will know what a pathetically wee thing it looked, for it was produced indeed in much weakness and while I was still struggling with the problem associated with daily living.

We must now go back a little in order to get the right approach

to the publishing of *The Berean Expositor*. For a period of a-
bout eighteen months, regular studies had been held in the
home of Mr. Brininger, with increasing light and conviction.
One shackle after another fell from us and we began to appreciate what it was to be free. As the number that attended
these meetings remained small, and as we felt that we had a
message to give that demanded a wider circle of hearers, it
was at length decided to put the subject into print, so toward
the close of the year 1908, and just before the interview with
Dr. Bullinger, the first number was prepared. Among other
things that had to be settled was the title that we were going
to give to the new publication. I wanted particularly to include the word "Expositor" for it was the exposition of the
Scriptures that had been laid upon my heart and conscience,
but I could not get any supplementary title that was satisfactory.

It was my custom in those days to attend the services at the
Metropolitan Tabernacle, and I remember discussing this
question of the title with the lady who subsequently became my
wife and helpmeet, but we arrived at no conclusion except
that "Expositor" must form part of the name.

The preacher that evening was Archibald Brown, and his
text "The nobility of the Bereans". I had found my title. The
magazine must be called *The Berean Expositor*, and I wrote,
and acquainted Archibald Brown with the outcome of the sermon. In the early and happy days of the Bible Training College, concerning which we have already written, a welcome
visiting teacher was Mr. George E. Page, whose lectures on
"The attributes of God" were a wonderful help to a young beginner. In the year 1947 (that is forty years afterward) Mr
Page wrote to me, having come across some of my writings,
and remembered the name of the young man who was always so
full of questions. Mr. Page had compiled a summary of the
life of Archibald Brown to mark the centenary of his birth in
1844, and told me that he still possessed the pulpit diary used
by Archibald Brown on that Sunday in December 1908, wherein he noted his subject "The nobility of the Bereans". This
was a happy combination of remembrances, both of an old and
respected teacher and of the incident so intimately connected
with the naming of the magazine. The ministry of Archibald
Brown at the Metropolitan Tabernacle lasted from June 16th,
1907 until December 18th, 1910, and the closing entries in his
diary read:

Ephesians 3:21   "Unto Him be glory"

Acts 20:24   "The Ministry Received"
and the reader will see a peculiar significance in these texts
as they think of the nobility of the Bereans, and *The Berean*

Expositor although of course Archibald Brown to the end of his days was a Calvinistic Baptist. The first page of the first number of *The Berean Expositor* opens the witness with the following headlines:

Acts 28: 17-31

ITS BEARING UPON THE PRESENT DISPENSATION

An introductory study to prepare the way for future expositions on vital dispensational subjects.

We have travelled far since these words were printed in February, 1909, and some of our findings have been modified and expanded, but this great Dispensational Landmark, and its bearing upon the two groups of Paul's epistles, has been the chart and compass of all our subsequent teaching, and all our subsequent exposition has been but the logical outcome of this one great fact. If we have contributed nothing of value since, we believe that this note which was then struck was a note in harmony with the Divine Purpose; and we have had the joy of knowing that in spite of weakness and great opposition, that note has sounded round the whole world, and that numbers in every continent bless the day when first they heard the joyful sound. In subsequent articles, the biographical character of this series will give place to the doctrinal, and we hope to trace the Lord's unfolding of His truth during the intervening years. It will be impossible, however, not to refer at times to personal circumstances for these are as much interwoven with the revelation of the Mystery, as the early epistles of Paul are interwoven with the history of the Acts period.

I WENT INTO ARABIA

The endeavour to qualify as an Art Master, and so be able to earn a decent living, accompanied as it was by lack of funds, and necessarily poor living, ultimately collapsed when a revisal of the qualifications necessary to gain the Art Master Certificate was introduced and all hope of continuing long enough to succeed ended. Mr. Edwin S. Taylor, a co-secretary of the Bible Training College was a Commercial Artist in 68, Fleet Street, where the offices of the Bible Training College were, and he kindly offered me a post and the £2 per week which I immediately received seemed "wealth, beyond the dreams of avarice". Just before this, meetings had been convened by readers of *Things to Come* at the Holborn Town

Hall, not far from the ancient timbered Staple Inn, where two hundred gathered on a Sunday evening for some time.

Staple Inn. Elizabethan. C.H.W.

At their commencement my affairs were in such a state that to reach that meeting my dear one (afterward, my beloved wife) walked with me from South East London and back, while some who attended the meetings arrived and returned by cab. At length Mr Leonard Pinkney called a meeting, explained the circumstances and my out of pocket expenses were met. The work I did at the Drawing Office was mainly two-fold:

1. Most exact and minute drawing on box-wood blocks, of surgical instruments, for the making of wood engravings and
2. The retouching of photographs of machinery, which involved the spraying of white lead.

To counter the poisonous effects of white lead, milk had to be taken daily. I felt a little like the cleaner and dyer who put up the sign "We dye to live", but was nevertheless thankful that my long quest was over.

I can now see that the four years gaining Art Qualification was my "Arabia". I was being tested to see how long I would resist the invitations to "soft pedal" the truth, and discontinue *The Berean Expositor* Only grace sufficient, abundantly supplied, and the loyalty of a handful of fellow believers enabled me to "stand and withstand".

In 1913 Dr. Bullinger finished his course, and his last words written for the *Companion Bible* were those of John 10:14, 15 (*below):

HIS AND HIS FATHER'S KNOWLEDGE.   Introversion.

```
 *    h 14- I am the good Shepherd
      i-14- And I know My sheep
      k-14 And am known of Mine
      k 15- As the Father knoweth Me
      i -15- even so know I the Father
     h-15 And I lay down My life for the sheep.
```

His rough notes were sufficient for his co-editors to complete the Gospel of John, but after that, they were faced with a problem.

The awakening of the Berean Spirit (Acts 17:11).

"*The Berean Expositor* stands for unhesitating investigation and undaunted publication of the testimony of the infallible Word of God. The Editor and his colleagues are human, but they seek grace to continue regardless of human opinions. If the truth is desired the magazine will continue, if the truth is not needed the magazine has no further warrant for existence.

While valuing the fellowship of all like-minded believers, *The Berean Expositor* will continue untrammelled. It is the organ of no society, it is the property of no sect, it is the exponent of no creed. It is a searcher of Scripture".

see page 87

It must be admitted that there is something pugnacious about this extract from the Foreword to Volume 1, re-issued in 1914, but there is a history and a reason behind it as the reader can well imagine.

Three days after his conversion, and immediately after the gracious visit of Ananias, Paul passed through an experience which in the language of The Acts reads:

"And immediately there fell from his eyes *as it had been scales*" (Acts 9:18).

Paul was well-stored with the letter of the Word, he was called to be an apostle, he was filled with holy spirit, and the scales fell from his eyes "immediately". Alas, in my case, I had no such store of Scripture truth, not even the mere letter of the Word; I received no Apostolic call, neither was I filled with the spirit! Seven years, not three days intervened between my conversion and liberation. In my case no Ananias came and called me "brother", but alone, with no one to help or to guide except the Lord and His Word, the scales fell, immediately the same spirit was exercised that prompted the Bereans "to search and see if it were so". If my road to Damascus was Exeter Hall, my parallel with Acts 9:18 was in the privacy of my room seven years later.

I have sketched very lightly in the earlier articles of this series, both the occasion of my conversion and the subsequent Secretaryship of the Training College that covered the years 1904 to 1908. In that sketch the reader will have seen that I had no Christian upbringing, no Bible knowledge, not even a traditional or formal faith. It was not surprising therefore that I eagerly absorbed teaching that appeared to have the sanction both of Scripture and of scholarship.

As time went on and the knowledge of the Scriptures increased, increasing light began to have its liberating effect, but any move in the direction of liberty of thought or independent opinion was held in with a tight rein. Over and over again when I expressed a difference of opinion regarding a doctrine, an interpretation or a principle of action, my search for light was checked by the suggestion that I should "pray about it" with the very obvious implication, that to dare to differ from the teaching of the leader was something beyond argument. However, certain passages from Ephesians having come up in the course of routine study, were ever in the background, until there came a day when I dared to differ strongly on some item of teaching. Coupled with this the discontinuance of the Training College work, and the taking up with the idea of founding a "primitive church" led at length to the severance already spoken of.

One of the lessons I then learned and one that I have never since forgotten, was the danger of leaning upon another, however qualified and advanced that other might be. It was the dawning of the Berean spirit, although unrecognised at the time. After one such painful conference, when much that I had originally accepted snapped under the strain of criticism, I made a mental vow that never again would I accept from any man, whoever he may be, any teaching as Truth until I had made it my own after rigorous and thorough searching of the Word. The Berean spirit came out into the realm of recognised experience in the following way.

Among the unquestioned teachings that had up till then been received, was that which is expressed in the words "The Seven Parables of Matthew 13". Not only had the parables been expounded and explained, a parallel had been instituted to show the close relationship between them and "the Seven Churches" of the Apocalypse. Book after book, pamphlet after pamphlet proclaimed with awe-inspiring unity "There are SEVEN parables in Matthew 13", and the idea of even questioning the statement or of counting the parables never entered the mind. It was as though one might as well question the existence of the sun and the moon! One such book which I still possess has the statement "The seventh and LAST parable", shutting the mind up to the idea of seven and seven only. Incidentally one of the favourite interpretations of these parables, was to imply, without actually asserting, that we were approaching the ecclesiastical position of the "Pearl" which found a parallel in the "Philadelphian" Church, after which of course there was nothing left but Laodicea and apostacy.

My emancipation from the thraldom of man, to the glorious freedom of believing only and all that the Scripture shall be found to teach is intimately connected with Matthew 13 and its "seven" parables, which must explain and excuse my dwelling at such length upon this feature. I can remember the occasion most vividly, although more than fifty years have since passed. I had taken up my pen and had written across the top of a sheet of paper the legend "Seven Parables of Matthew 13", and was about to put together a few notes to help me to speak on the passage at a Bible meeting, when I reminded myself that I had resolved never to take anything for granted any more. I must confess I felt somewhat foolish at pausing to consider the obvious, but nevertheless I did actually count the parables of Matthew 13. To my amazement, and my joy, the very first attempt at independent research was rewarded. There were EIGHT parables. From one point of view the whole thing is trivial in the extreme, but from another angle that discovery was a crisis.

All the teaching of the past few years suddenly became suspect. It may have been doctrinally sound in many of its tenets, but it was fundamentally unsound in its spirit. It "savoured" of men. With the counting of the parables for myself a new epoch had arrived; the Berean spirit had vindicated itself.

The consequences of this simple act were both immediate and far-reaching. The immediate effect was a completely new understanding of the purpose of Matthew 13. The far-reaching effect can be seen on every page of this magazine for the period of over fifty years. In this somewhat personal account of the discovery and presentation of Dispensational Truth, we hope to present to the reader not only the bare truth itself, but where it is pertinent and profitable to show how certain positions were reached with their consequences.

In the present article we have but introduced the theme and must limit our presentation by showing the first personal discovery in the realm of Dispensational Truth, as revealed in these parables of the Mysteries of the Kingdom of Heaven.

We give the following extract from *The Berean Expositor*
Vol. XXlll pp. 202-204:

"The result was so illuminating, and the blow to traditional teaching so palpable, that not only did it prove the com-
mandment that 'came' to the one upon whose convictions
we are now commenting, but it settled for ever the policy
of the Editor as to all subsequent investigations.
"Instead of seven parables, Matthew 13 contains eight.
These are arranged in perfect symetry, and form the only
true basis for their exposition. Whoever has once seen
this perfect correspondence realizes that no amount of
erudition or ability will ever compensate for its omission".

THE EIGHT PARABLES OF MATTHEW 13.

A 1-9   THE SOWER   The sowing of the seed into four kinds
of ground.
13. They (Israel) did *not* understand.
B 24-30   THE TARES   Good and bad together. Separated at
the harvest (the end of the age); the bad
are cast into a furnace of fire, there
shall be wailing and gnashing of teeth.
C 31,32   THE MUSTARD TREE   One tree.
D 33   THE LEAVEN   Hid in three measures of meal.

*These first four parables spoken outside the house to great
multitudes.*

D 44   THE TREASURE   Hid in a field.
C̄ 45,46   GOODLY PEARLS   One pearl.
B̲ 47-50   THE DRAG NET   Good and bad together. Separated
at the end of the age; the bad are cast
into a furnace of fire, there shall be
wailing and gnashing of teeth.
51. They (disciples) *did* understand.
A 52   THE SCRIBE   The treasure opened to those in the house.

*These last four parables were spoken inside the house to the
disciples.*

It is not our purpose to give an exposition of these parables.
We content ourselves here with their place in this testimony.
One positive feature that gave added weight to this interpretation of the parables, however, must be included. We observed
that not until the Lord was evidently rejected (Matt. 11:12) did
the word "mystery" appear upon the pages of Scripture, and
that it is coupled with a very solemn quotation from Isaiah 6:10.
An examination of The Acts of the Apostles shows that as Israel in the *land* rejected their Messiah, so did Israel of the
dispersion and therefore Acts 28 stands to the wider testimony

that Matthew does to the people of the land. In Acts 28 Israel fail, and evidently miracles cease. This failure is anticipated in Matthew 11:20-24 and 13:58. There in Acts 28 as in Matthew 13, Isaiah 6:10 is solemnly quoted, and immediately after the rejection of Israel which then took place "mystery" again follows, this time, not the mystery of the kingdom of heaven, but the dispensation of the mystery as made known to Paul, the Lord's prisoner.

"We gather from this testimony that one of the greatest hindrances to full acceptance of the truth is the blinding power of tradition, that confused kingdom with church, and does not recognize the true place of the gospel of the kingdom in the purpose of the Ages. We commend this testimony to all who seek to know 'what is the dispensation of the mystery' (Eph. 3:9 R. V.)".

At the request of Dr. Bullinger I supplied the structure of these eight parables for use in the *Companion Bible* It can be seen in Appendix 145.

We now return to the extract from the Foreword of Volume 1, trusting that the reader will more readily and more sympathetically understand the extremely independent attitude which is there indicated.

In this frame of mind and in this spirit, the witness was conceived. In this selfsame spirit it has grown, and when the Berean spirit that gave it birth wanes, the witness of *The Berean Expositor* will cease.

The following appeared in the *News-Chronicle* of October 21st, 1949. Some of the statements need a little revision; my father fought hard for free education; and religious opposition made him rebellious and sceptical. He would not have recognised the title "Anarchist". However, as these are the last public utterances of the Doctor we preserve it as a testimony.

"Bermondsey paid affectionate tribute yesterday afternoon to 'our Doctor', Dr. Scott Lidgett, founder of the Bermondsey Settlement, from the wardenship of which he has just retired. And Dr. Lidgett, who is aged 95, paid tribute to Bermondsey.

'Never suppose', he said, 'that the people of Bermondsey must be treated as stupid or as capable of appreciating only inferior gifts. Set before them your pearls of greatest price'.

He told of a young man - an agnostic whose parents were almost anarchists, through his Greek studies in the settlement, had been converted, and who had then converted his father and mother".

The thirteenth chapter of Matthew is the dispensational

landmark of the Lord's earthly ministry. The rejection that reaches a climax in Matthew 11:29-30 is followed by the introduction of "mystery" in Matthew 13, the quotation of Isaiah 6: 9, 10 and a reference back to something that had been kept secret *from* the foundation of the world. The next great step in the recovery of long-lost truth was the recognition of the importance of another landmark, namely Acts 28, which followed the pattern of Matthew 11-13 on a larger scale. There once again the rejection of the Messiah by Israel reaches a climax, there for the last time Isaiah 6:9, 10 is quoted, and in the epistle to the Ephesians, written while Paul was a prisoner at Rome, there is a reference back to something that had been kept secret from *before* the foundation of the world.

The first words which I wrote in the interest of Dispensational Truth that appeared in print, are to be found in *The Berean Expositor* of February 1909, Volume 1 page 1.

In April 1909 under the heading "Dispensational Expositions" a similar article, with a similar heading appears in *Things to Come*. With this opening article a series commenced which continued until 1915 when publication ceased. Two articles had appeared before this one, in March 1909 being signed and entitled "The Unity of the Spirit" (Eph. 4:3) "What is it?" the other, unsigned appearing in February 1909, entitled "Rightly Dividing the Word of Truth as to the Lord's Coming". These two articles were written as a foreword to the more systematic treatment of the subject that commenced in April 1909.
The articles that ran through *Things to Come* from April to December 1909, bore the following titles:

Acts 28:17-31.
The Dispensational Position before Acts 28.
The Earlier Pauline Epistles.
Pentecost and the Mystery. (This article has been reprinted and is published at the price of 2/- per dozen).
1 Corinthians and Hebrews 5 and 6.
The Six-fold Foundation of Hebrews.
Hebrews 6 in the Light of the Epistle as a Whole.

During the same period, the first volume of *The Berean Expositor* was in course of production, and the same dispensational studies were prepared for both magazines. Other issues were raised which formed no part of my witness in Things to Come, and these must be given due consideration, but for the moment we are concerned with the opening note that was sounded on the front page.

Unless a writer from the very first received his message by inspiration of God, we should expect to discover occasions when a position once occupied had to be given up and if, moreover, we add to the handicap that such a writer was a pioneer, whose path was cluttered with "much rubbish" (Neh. 4:10), whose problems alas were as much concerning the bread that perisheth as they were concerning the truth of God, and who could only offer the closing hours of a weary day to the Lord for His use, then perhaps the wonder will be, not that there were occasions when steps had to be retraced, but that they were on the whole so few and slight. With regard to the dispensational importance of Acts 28 this was clearly seen at once, seen as a whole, and seen with most of its logical consequences as they had a bearing upon the hope of the Church, the ordinances, the order of the epistles and the two-fold ministry of Paul.

The bearing upon the epistles of Paul was, as we have already said, the burden of an interview with Dr. Bullinger, so graciously and readily admitted by him. Throughout the succeeding years, Acts 28 has been the pole star that has set the course of all my interpretation. No criticism which we have yet received has touched the essential truth of the position then adopted, and much important teaching has come to light as a legitimate and logical outcome of that early vision that but adds confirmation. One of the reasons for the preparation of this series, is, that it appears wise and necessary after the lapse of years, to indicate for the benefit of any who shall investigate the grounds of our teaching, that they may have first hand information concerning the position arrived at after the sifting process of the years has been accomplished.

The importance which I attached to the bearing of Acts 28 was expressed on the first page of *The Berean Expositor* thus:

"Just as a stick appears bent when standing in the water, so our understanding of Scripture will be distorted whilst we ignore the differing media. In other words, if we stand in the dispensation of the Mystery, and try to act as though we were in the dispensation of the Kingdom, we shall in "that day" if not here, be ashamed, through not rightly dividing the Word of Truth".

A frontier or a boundary may be of itself an arid, unproductive area, of little value for its own sake, but of extreme value by reason of what is reserved and marked off from other surrounding territories. Acts 28 assumed its extreme importance to me when I pondered its bearing upon the doctrine, calling and hopes of the epistles that were written on either side of that dividing line. This led me to question the teaching given by Dr. Bullinger in his book *The Church Epistles*. On page 21 of the second edition is set out the seven epistles to the churches. We reproduce the arrangement of these epistles for the benefit of any reader who may not have access to Dr. Bullinger's works.

THE SEVEN EPISTLES TO THE CHURCHES.

A ROMANS. "Doctrine and Instruction". The Gospel of God: never hidden, "promised afore". God's justification of Jew and Gentile individually - dead and risen with Christ (1-8). Their relation dispensationally (9-11). The subjective foundation of the mystery.

B CORINTHIANS. "Reproof". *Practical* failure to exhibit the teaching of Romans through not seeing their standing as having died and risen with Christ. "Leaven" in practice (1 Cor. 5:6).

C GALATIANS. "Correction". *Doctrinal* failure as to the teaching of Romans. Beginning with the truth of the new nature ("spirit") they were soon removed (1:6), and sought to be made perfect in the old nature ("flesh") (3:3). "Leaven" in doctrine (5:9).

A EPHESIANS. "Doctrine and Instruction". The Mystery of God, always hidden, never before revealed. Jews and Gentiles collectively made "one new man" in Christ. Seated in the heavenlies with Christ.

B PHILIPPIANS. "Reproof". Practical failure to exhibit the teaching of Ephesians in manifesting "the mind of Christ" as members of the one Body.

C COLOSSIANS. "Correction". Doctrinal failure as to the teaching of Ephesians. Wrong doctrines which come from "not holding the Head" (2:19) and not seeing their completeness and perfection in Chrsit (2:8-10).

A THESSALONIANS. "Doctrine and Instruction". Not only "dead and risen with Christ" (as in Romans); not only seated in the heavenlies with Christ (as in Ephesians); but "caught up to meet the Lord in the air, so to be for ever with the Lord". In Romans, justified in Christ; in Ephesians, sanctified in Christ; in Thessalonians glorified with Christ. No "reproof". No "correction". All praise and thanksgiving. A typical church.

It will be seen that Thessalonians comes last, and is looked upon as the crown and climax of both Romans and Ephesians.

"Not only seated in the heavenlies with Christ (as in Ephesians); but "caught up to meet the Lord in the air, so to be for ever with the Lord".

Following this outline is the comment:

"And now we see another reason why Thessalonians comes

last. There are no epistles beyond this, because there is no higher truth to be taught. The consummation is reached".

This was the issue which was raised at that critical interview with the Doctor in 1908, where, although he had written the above, he was gracious enough to admit that there was fuller light dawning and did not despise the exceedingly earthen vessel through which the gleam shone. Believing that the record of the Acts supplies the time and place, and that the epistles written during the period contain the doctrine, calling and hope that was true dispensationally for that same time, I felt that it was impossible to end with Thessalonians in this way. Accordingly when the interview at Bury Street took place, the following outline taken from Volume 1, page 83 was suggested:

1 Thessalonians	A. D. 52	
2 Thessalonians	A. D. 53	Pentecostal and Transitional
1 Corinthians	A. D. 57	Period. Kingdom truth and
2 Corinthians	A. D. 57	preparatory teaching by Paul
Galatians	A. D. 57	for the impending change.
Romans	A. D. 58	
Acts 28:25-27.	A. D. 62	The Dispensational Boundary.
Ephesians	A. D. 62	Prison
Colossians	A. D. 62	Prison
Philippians	A. D. 62	Prison The dispensation of
1 Timothy	A. D. 67	Prison the Mystery-Standard
Titus	A. D. 67	truth for the time.
2 Timothy	A. D. 68	Prison

This, as the reader will see, is imperfect, Philemon and Hebrews are omitted and Galatians occurs late in the first list. These items were reviewed and replaced as fuller light was given. The arrangement of the epistles as set out above is not accurate nor complete and is not here printed for anything intrinsic in itself, but for the new approach that it heralds.

Epistles must not be grouped according to the individual fancy of the expositor, therefore the attempt, even though inaccurate in some details was made to deal with the epistles chronologically, believing that by so doing, we would better perceive what is "Truth for the Times". In another article we shall have to show how it came about that Galatians was placed first in the list, and that the epistle to the Hebrews was given a place before Acts 28.

"Seeing then that we have such hope, we use great plainness of speech" (2 Cor. 3:12).

I

The reader who has followed this history will have realized by now, that the witness of *The Berean Expositor* could hardly have been more insignificant in its commencement, but that lowly as its origin may have been, the nature of its teaching was likely to arouse opposition rather than receive much help. Human nature being what it is, we can but look back with amazement at the grace that must have been given, not only enabling us to be willing to stand alone, and to risk almost complete isolation for our pains, but to resist the temptation to omit or disguise some of the features of the new witness which would be offensive to many orthodox believers.

Perhaps no one piece of teaching so completely cut us off, both from fellowship and possible help, as the articles that were published in the opening volume, on the dispensational place of the Lord's Supper. Before that volume was published, doors of service were open to us, doors that we knew would most certainly close the moment the position we had taken up became public, and the temptation to listen to the voice of expediency, "opportunities for service must not be thrown away, etc. etc." when spoken in the ear of one who was at the time struggling, at the age of thirty, to make a fresh start in life was strong indeed.

I cannot be too thankful that the temptation "to soft pedal" was resisted, and that I was able to follow however "far off" in the footsteps of the great Apostle who said:

"Therefore, seeing we have this ministry, as we have received mercy, we faint not; But having renounced the hidden things of dishonesty, not walking in craftiness, nor handling the Word of God deceitfully; but by manifestation of the truth commending ourselves to every man's conscience in the sight of God". (2 Cor. 4:1, 2).

The reader will probably know that we base our attitude on the Lord's Supper squarely upon its Scriptural relationship with the New Covenant. We saw that there could be no possible connection between a new covenant made with the self same people that had broken the old covenant, and a mystery that had been hidden from the ages and generations, and not revealed until Israel had been set aside in Acts 28. One of the greatest objections to our position was the fact that the Lord's Supper was to be observed "till He come", and the meeting of this objection naturally raised a second question, namely that of the Second Coming, with its connection with the hope of Israel, the manifestation in glory; and the use of the term *parousia.* As a sequel to this, the place of water baptism was considered, so that we were literally asking for ostracism.

"Churchianity" as distinct from "Christianity" could expect no help from *The Berean Expositor* and conversely, by taking Dispensational Truth to its logical conclusion, *The Berean Expositor* must of necessity find many opponents among the orthodox, and did in fact lose many erstwhile supporters.

Yet this was not all. A further test of loyalty remained. Not only were we seeing light upon the place of Baptism and the Lord's Supper that rendered our witness "dangerous" in the eyes of many, we were also seeing light upon the nature of the soul, hell, and the wages of sin that was indeed "damnable heresy" in the estimation of others. Looking back at those perilous days, considering the frailty of the earthen vessel, and the ever present temptation "Command these stones that they be made *bread*", we can only marvel at the grace that saved the smoking flax from extinction, and record it here for the encouragement of any who may be at the cross roads in their ministry.

In the early numbers of Volume 1, we commenced an enquiry into the question of the immortality of the soul, and the words translated "for ever", and then in the last issue of the first volume there was commenced a series that ran through Volumes 2, 3 and 4, entitled "The wages of Sin".

For the greater part of my Christian life up till this time, I had lived under the necessity to put attendance at the Lord's Table among the first claims upon my time and strength, allowing neither the claims of humanity, holiday or personal affairs to intervene; I had also lived under the dreadful belief that the Scriptures taught the eternal conscious suffering of every man, woman or child who was not a believer in Christ and which awful fate some with whom I met, secretly believed awaited many so-called orthodox Christians! To be labelled by an assembly "a non-eternity man" was to taste the dregs of bitterness. Were we willing to stoop so low? Should I not "postpone" the study or at least its publication "for a more convenient season"? After prayer, and consultation with the lady who became my wife, and who was soon to share a life-long fellowship of ostracism, yet of triumphant faith, and with the equally loyal support of Mr. Brininger I accepted the burden and its consequences and we decided to burn our boats.

The findings of those early days have since been made the basis of the booklet *"Hell, or Pure from the blood of all men"*, and we rejoice to know that some of the choicest saints of our acquaintance give ready testimony to the emancipating power of the truth there set forth. While the dispensational position of Acts 28 and of the epistle to the Ephesians and its logical consequences was uppermost in that early ministry, together with the doctrine of the soul and with the teaching of the Scripture concerning Hell, there runs through the first volume the thin red line of expositions that touch at several points the great Sacrifice of the Saviour's love. The very titles are suggestive: "Christ our Surety"; "Clean every whit"; Sanctification, its connexion with the atonement, resurrection and likeness to Christ"; The Whole Burnt Offering"; "Wondrous meeting places" (Isa. 53); and "Does Particular redemption exhaust the sacrifice of Christ"?

Even in that early day I saw that the judgment of the great white throne was twofold and quoted the rendering of J. N. D. and of J. R. Rotherham "And if *anyone* was not found written in the book of life *he was* cast into the lake of fire", and followed the quotations with the comment "Instead of the orthodox idea of myriads being cast into the lake of fire, Scripture leads us to see that it is to be an intensely individual matter, depending not upon works, but upon the book of life".

Our study of the Word drove us to the conclusion that the soul of man is not inherently immortal, that immortality is a gift in grace conferred at the resurrection; that the dead are asleep, that they awake at the resurrection, and that there is no conscious intermediate state. The wages of sin is death, and John 3:16 puts before us the alternatives of "perishing" and of "life everlasting".

The last of this series of studies lifts the subject above the realm of private interpretation, by giving a concordance of every word used in the controversy, and at the conclusion of the fifth article we quoted the words of Dr. Weymouth:

"My mind fails me to conceive a grosser misinterpretation of language than when the five or six strongest words which the Greek tongue possesses, signifying 'destroy' or 'destruction' are explained to mean, an everlasting but wretched existence. To translate black as white is nothing to this".

Thus the stage was set, the terms defined, and from these humble beginnings have arisen all that the witness of *The Berean Expositor* means to God and to His people, and to its author.

While it is by no means easy for me to write of these intimate and personal things, it is even more difficult to open my heart and speak as I should of the closest and dearest relationship of all. Owing to circumstances that have already been hinted at, I was engaged to be married for twelve years, and the loyalty, patience, love and simple faith of the beloved partner of my joys and sorrows, my fights and my fears, demand a tribute from me here, however I may falter in the rendering of it. I am however partly relieved of this very personal matter by the receipt of a letter, which says in the language of an observer, something of what I feel and would like to include in this survey.

A friend who saw these articles in manuscript form wrote a letter, one page of which we extract and print here.

"However difficult your early days - how wonderfully blest you were to have been given such a partner as Mrs Welch - what a joy to see her receive her reward for all the years of toil and sacrifice in so many ways; readiness to aid in the most difficult and laborious part of the work - cleaning the chapel at the commencement, caring and looking after the most difficult little ones at the school, carrying heavy bags of eats to the Chapel, suffering much loneliness as she must have done in the early years - always seeing you had your best bib and tucker when going on your visits, sending you off with her blessing and upholding you in prayer whilst away. You may be - and are - a remarkable man, but you have an equally remarkable wife. I repeat, *nothing* is lost, she is a splendid witness to all Christian women, of a life of sacrifice - patience with such a man as yourself, which must needs surpass that of Job sometimes " and labours beyond her physical strength.

God bless you both abundantly,
Yours, tremendously privileged to know both
(Signed) . . . .

"DISPENSATIONAL TRUTH" and the "REGIONS BEYOND".

We have already shown that some of our publications were prepared and issued in order that our position regarding certain vital issues should be clear to friend and foe alike. These booklets were *"The Deity of Christ"*, *" The Reconciliation of All Things"* and *"Sin and its Relation to God"*. The reader is sensible from the first page that these booklets were written in the midst of controversy and were the product of contention for the faith. *The Berean Expositor* itself also was the product of necessity. I had no "urge" to write as some authors and writers have admitted - indeed, had I followed my bent I should have been an artist, but "necessity was laid upon me" and there was nothing for it but to launch out into the deep and put the message that had been entrusted into print. Never have I written or published *The Berean Expositor* just because I felt I would like to edit "a religious magazine", for by so doing I spoiled my worldly prospects, used up time and strength without remuneration and without recognition, receiving in-

sults where one might have expected gratitude, and experienced ostracism and loneliness while explaining the fellowship
of the Mystery.
"*Dispensational Truth*", a book of some 300 pages, was issued in the year 1912. It was the firstborn of three similar
volumes and it made its entry into the world when the author
was almost at his wits end to obtain the bread that perisheth.
Most if not every one of Paul's epistles were elicited by the
immediate needs of the churches. It is evident that he did not
sit down and intentionally write a treatise or a book. In like
manner "*Dispensational Truth*" was conceived. I did not take
up the pen and say to myself I will write a book and call it
Dispensational Truth. It came about in a more homely way.
A young man, whose mother had come into the light, and who
had opened her home for meetings along the lines of Dispensational Truth, paid me a visit, and for several hours asked
questions and received answers. At the çlose of the long interview he said "Why don't you put all this into a book? There
must be many like myself who would appreciate such a work".
I just told him simply and frankly that it was a matter of
money. I would gladly do the work, but I had not a single penny
in the world to spend on such an undertaking. He said he felt
sure that he could raise the amount needed among his friends.
In this he proved to be too sanguine, but his enthusiasm was
fruitful, for at a meeting held subsequently at my parent's
house in Denmark Park, a promise of £50 was made by those
there gathered, and with this as an earnest I prepared to write
the book.

Before a line could be written I was obliged to enter hospital and undergo an operation - which I am thankful to say was
successful - but which left me in the predicament that I could
only stand up or lie down. A brother in the Lord kindly invited me to spend a few weeks at his home in Sunningdale,
Berkshire, and there I spent my convalescence,   *standing*
at a desk writing a few pages, or *lying prone* on the grass
outside to get over the strain.

The following note in *The Berean Expositor* for June 1911
reads, "Editor's Proposed Book. - We are pleased to be able
to acknowledge the following donations ...... these sums together with promised donations and the approximate value of
advance orders for copies amount to £37, so we are encouraged to believe that the work is desired. £38 is still needed,
and of course we shall not place the MSS in the printer's hands
until the full amount is assured". These sums of money now
seem trifling, but in 1911 and in my then financial position
they seemed wealth. From such poor and insignificant beginnings can the Lord in His grace produce a harvest if He

so wills. When "*Dispensational Truth*" was at length issued in 1912, I sent a copy to the surgeon who had performed the operation. He wrote from Upper Wimpole Street, W., saying:

> "... I am glad to hear that the operation was a complete success and did not interfere with your labours. The latter must have been stupendous.
>
> Yours sincerely,
>
> P. M. H. "

I have often wondered what effect the book had and where that individual copy is now. In the Preface to the work occur the words:

> "Its production, whether viewed from the financial standpoint or the stand-point of actual labour, is the result of much self-sacrifice and loving fellowship".

The whole of the MSS was passed on to Mr. Brininger, who rose early and worked for an hour or so each day before setting out for daily business, and so produced the type-script for the printer. The reading of proofs and the whole of the business side largely fell upon him whether the accounts with the printer or the despatch of orders when the book was finished.

Among those who wrote to express interest in the volume was one very near the Royal family in Russia. Countess Leiven, who was among the nobility massacred in the Bolshevik uprising, was a reader of *Things to Come* and a believer in the Word Rightly Divided, and while I did not receive many such letters, there are evidences that in other high ranks of society, humble members of the One Body were to be found.

While the exceedingly limited nature of our work and the extremely unpopular teaching which was its mission to make known, deprived us of help that might otherwise have been received from Bible lovers and evangelical believers, some work was accomplished in "the regions beyond" our own immediate circle and it is a joy to record in these latter years, a ministry that extends, literally, to the ends of the earth.

I received a letter asking whether I could supply material for many gaps that were in the structure of the Acts which Dr. Bullinger had left unfinished. Seeing that the last member Acts 28:23-31, was not given its distinctive place, but split into two sections, I supplied a complete structure, along the lines found in *From Pentecost to Prison* on page 3 but this was rejected.

Mr. Wm. Barron of New Zealand who had suggested the

Companion Bible to Dr. Bullinger and largely financed it, immediately upon receiving news of the Doctor's death sent a cable "Put Welch on to the Epistles". This too was rejected, one of the reasons being "he would ruin the sales". Most likely I would have done, but that was not the real objection. The co-editors adopted the canon "We do not know what Dr. Bullinger *would have written* we can only go back and adopt what he has already written" although his last book" *The Foundations of Dispensational Truth* " makes it clear that he fully accepted Acts 28 as the Dispensational Boundary and the segregation of "The Prison Epistles". I quote one or two extracts which should be read together with the above comments.

> "In regard to *"Things to Come"* you have confirmed what I have been saying to my friends here that *"Things to Come"* is going back ever since the Dr's Editorials and supervision stopped. Take your articles out of *"Things to Come"* and we have gone back quite ten years".

Another letter dated 25th March 1919

> "Had Miss Dodson fallen in with our request that you should be identified with Mr. Bowker in the *Companion Bible* work all the present trouble which has arisen would not have occurred".

In another letter dealing rather with the financial features of the *Companion Bible* Mr. Barron said:

> "I have given you all this information, believing that you would already have been identified with this work had those who have had to do with the finance been honoured in this matter".

Another believer wrote about the same time:

> "We are glad to hear of your connection with the *Companion Bible* This sets our minds at rest as to the lines on which that volume will be completed".

Responding to a suggestion from the co-editor, I prepared twenty four appendices in connexion with Paul's epistles. These were acknowledged but never used. The reader may be interested to see the titles of these rejected appendices, and perhaps see the reasons that prompted their rejection.

APPENDIXES

1. *The place of Abraham in the Epistles of Paul.*
2. *Chronological order of Paul's Epistles.*
3. *Parallels between Ephesians and Colossians.*
4. *Parallels between Philippians and 2 Timothy.*
5. *The dispensational bearing of Isaiah 6: 10.*
6. *The Pentecostal Dispensation neither permanent nor continuous.*
7. *The difference between the Epistles of "Pentecost" and the omission or inclusion of certain words..*

8. *"Gifts" in the Church.*
9. *The "Body" in 1 Cor. 12:1, Rom. 12.*
10. *The usage of the word "Gospel" in Philippians.*
11. *"Circumcision" in the Epistles of the Mystery.*
12. *"Till He Come".*
    "That blessed hope" "the hope of glory"
    Parousia, Apocalypse, Epiphany.
13. *The evidential character of miracles.*
14. *The Mystery of Christ and the Mystery of the*
    present dispensation.
15. *The twofold ministry of Paul.*
16. *Reconciliation.*
17. *Ministry in the One Body.*
18. *The laying of hands.*
19. *The two orders of apostles.*
20. *"Godliness".*
21. *The Crown and the Prize.*
22. *Light upon Phil. 3 from a consideration of the*
    theme of the Epistles to the Hebrews.
23. *The resurrection of Christ as viewed in the "Acts" con-*
    trasted with the view of the epistles of the Mystery.
24. *O. T. quotations in the Epistles of Paul demonstrating*
    the new line of teaching revealed in Ephesians.

The following extract from a letter, written on April 17th, 1913 may not need a lengthy explanation, at least to some of our lady readers.

"What you said in your letter to-day seems scarcely possible. I think you had better make haste and give me the design for the frock or else it will be *that* keeping us waiting".

"That" refers to the fact that we were engaged to be married for twelve years, before the happy union was possible. While with Mr. Heward I was subjected to great pressure to give up all idea of marriage "for the Lord's sake", but although very uncertain of the Scriptural grounds for my choice, I continued to look forward to that day when that blessed partnership could be realized. We were married on July 30th 1914 at the Rotherham Free Church, and a few days later war broke out bringing with it further problems, but finding us at last yoked together.

The kindness of so many friends and readers when at last it became possible for us to get married was somewhat overwhelming, and the accompanying acknowledgement I feel should be preserved in this story of my early days. *(see next page)*

I have already recorded the accident that nearly proved fatal, when as a babe of fifteen months, I was scalded, and only saved under God by the skill and care of Guy's hospital doctors and nurses.

Four months after I was married, I was again placed in deadly peril, being involved in a railway accident that took a heavy toll of life. The local train leaving Ilford station for

PRESENTED TO Mr CHARLES HENRY WELCH BY FRIENDS IN LONDON
THE PROVINCES AND SCOTLAND, AS A TOKEN OF SINCERE
CHRISTIAN LOVE AND ESTEEM ON THE OCCASION OF HIS MARRIAGE
TO MISS WINIFRED JEANNETTE CLARK, JULY 30TH 1914.

INSCRIBED PLATE ON THE DESK

124, Cobham Rd,
South Park
Ilford Essex
Jan. 20th 1915.

Dear Friends
    Owing to the outbreak of war, following
immediately upon our marriage, delay has
been experienced in obtaining a full list
of those whose fellowship is depicted on
this page. My wife and myself, take this
belated opportunity of expressing our
sense of deep gratitude to all friends
for this token of love to us.
        Yours by immutable grace
              Charles H. Welch.

Liverpool St. was run into by an East coast express, which cut the local train in half, pitched the engine down an embankment, and crushed one carriage into splinters.

The carriage in which I travelled left the rails, turned on its side, and came to a grinding stop with a full complement of passengers compressed into about one third of normal space, with broken glass beneath and luggage, mats, and people, piled into a dreadful mix.

I escaped with but a small cut from broken glass, but was very conscious that once again I had been preserved, and that a Divine purpose was involved.

I could echo however faintly the sentiments of the apostle:

"Who delivered us from so great a death (*in the past*), and doth deliver us (*in the present*), and Whom we trust will yet deliver us (*in the future*)".

The double crossing of the Atlantic in 1955, together with 6700 miles travelling in the air, seems also to come within this "deliverance".

DOORS CLOSED AND DOORS OPENED
(Acts 16:6-12).

The continuance of the war brought the studio in Fleet Street to a close, after just two years exemption from penury.

Owing to medical rejection by the military authorities, and the warning by my doctor that:

"Working all day in a small closed room, with white lead spraying into the atmosphere, and working into the night on the *Berean Expositor* and preparation for meetings, I was heading for T.B. ", we removed into the country, and I found employment in the open air, working from six a.m. to late afternoon at a nursery in Rayleigh, Essex. The work was

rigorous and the going hard, but we had a large garden, many fruit trees, goats to supply all the milk needed, and we were sustained and kept.

There were several evident interventions of the Lord at this time that hedged my way and divided my paths. Realizing a drastic change was indicated if I was not to become a chronic invalid, or even worse leave my wife a widow, I early sought guidance as to the next step to take. A Gospel mission at Rayleigh, Essex was already familiar with the teaching of the *Berean Expositor* and on several occasions I had travelled out there to conduct the Sunday Services; I felt that Proverbs 3:5, 6 indicated that I should combine my search for health and house, with opportunity still to witness for the truth. The leading seemed to point to Rayleigh, so, accordingly I travelled out to this Essex village, spent the whole day prospecting for a suitable house, but returned to the railway station at night tired and unsuccessful.

As I sat waiting for the arrival of the train, a happy party of friends were saying their good-byes, and an elderly, sour looking man sitting beside me said, "some people are lucky to have such friends". I said something in the way of reply, and he further informed me that he was unhappy at his home, and was going to London to get away from his housekeeper and her son, who apparently were rather a worry. He then turned and said "You don't know anyone who wants to buy a house, do you? I want to sell mine, and I would give you £5 for finding a buyer. I quietly looked up to the Lord, (like Nehemiah 2:4, 5) and said "where is it?" He replied, "it is called Ebenezer Cottage, Hullbridge Road". This cottage was immediately opposite the lane leading to the Gospel Mission, but as it was not advertised for sale, I had passed it without a second thought. I said, "if I buy it myself do I get the £5?" He looked a bit surprised, but the upshot was, that after the kindly inspection of the building by our brother Wilfred Mills, I closed with the offer, and moved in. Our eldest child "Wyn" was then about six months old. For some time I worked in the nursery, producing food, mainly tomatoes and ultimately erected a set of greenhouses for my own use.

Again, the hand of the Lord was most evident, and demands an account of what happened here. The manager of the greenhouse where I had worked, came to me one day and said "are you still looking for some occupation to keep you here in the country?" I replied that I most certainly was, as the exchequer was exceedingly low and would soon be exhausted. He told me that at some distance away there were greenhouses for sale, to be taken down for rebuilding elsewhere. I visited them and estimated at current prices new material would cost about £800. These were going as they stood for £200. But here comes the most unbusinesslike move, that I felt, nevertheless, (with the agreement of my dear wife who so loyally stood by me all this time) I must make.

To appreciate the predicament I was in, and the nature of my action, it will be necessary to set out the disposition of the land on which my cottage and adjacent property stood. It will be seen that there was no means of access by cart, van or trolley, no room for stores, or for building greenhouses; the garden was full of fruit trees necessary for the household. Anyone with any common sense would have said "much as I would like to take advantage of this offer, it is quite out of the question, as I have nowhere to build them, and dare not waste the last £200 I possess on such a crazy venture". Nevertheless, believing that I was called "to go out not knowing" I wrote the cheque for £200 and became the possessor of this property. My financial resources were so limited that I lacked the face to go to one of the big banks, but had gone, very humbly, to Farrow's Bank in Cheapside, E. C. 2 where I opened an account on April 30th 1914 with a deposit of £124.10.0 The last entry in my pass book reads:

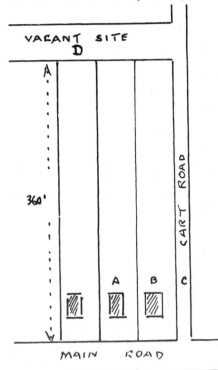

Dec. 31st, 1920. To Balance £41. 0.7.
The payment for the greenhouses was made on August 5th 1920.

Now comes the evidence of Providential overruling. Had I been very business like I should have lost, not only the balance £41. 0.7 which I did, but the £200 as well, for Farrow's Bank suddenly closed and ceased payment. I did at least have £200's worth of material. So for about three months, single-handed at odd times I removed three tons of glass, thousands of bricks and thousands of feet of timber, but still had no knowledge as to what to do with it all - until one day, the next Providential intervention occurred. The house adjoining Ebenezer (well named as it turned out) marked on the plan B, had a cart road at the side marked C and a piece of land running at right angles at the bottom marked D. This neighbour suddenly left England for a post in South Africa. I negotiated with his landlord, bought the piece of land marked D with my last ha'penny, and moved my £200 worth of material on to my own land, and commenced building in January 1921.

This range of greenhouses consisted of three houses built side by side, 150 ft. long and 12 ft. 6 ins. wide. I laid every brick, glazed every sash, cut every joint, painted the whole roof, and then with the assistance of a boy got the ground ready for planting, and sent a crop of tomatoes to London that weighed $4\frac{1}{2}$ tons! In all this arduous labour my dear wife, quite unaccustomed to country life, as I was myself, saw to goats for milking, chickens for eggs, and went inside the greenhouses and watered the plants with a hose six mornings a week while I worked a rotary pump by hand and used up my breakfast outside. One good thing resulted. We lived hard, but open air and hard labour, provoked a more healthy appetite, so that a strip had to be let in to the back of my waistcoat!

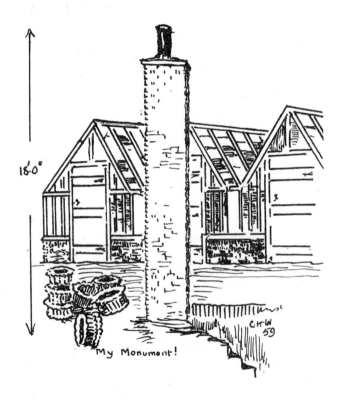

My Monument!

All this time it must be remembered that I was busy writing the articles for the *Berean Expositor* and wrote and produced with the kind assistance of Mr. F. P. Brininger, the volume entitled *The Apostle of the Reconciliation.*

Soon it became evident that I must do something to increase production, so among other Herculean tasks I sunk a well, built a chimney, and installed a tubular boiler and four inch pipes the whole length of the three houses. Later, with the assistance of a loan freely lent by Leonard Pinkney, I extended these houses another fifty feet each. But, although my produce received sometimes a trifle more than the top price advertised in the Trade Journal, I could not make a living.

First, because I was continually absent for the purpose of taking meetings in London, the Provinces and in Scotland, and second, because I was not distributing my costs by not employing labour. This led once more to a halt. I sat down with my wife in consultation and prayer:

"Either I must extend, and devote my whole time to *Tomatoes* or I must shut down and devote my whole time to the *Ministry*".

My dear wife, in face of possible and continual lack of means said: "there is no doubt what your *real* work is". That settled the matter, the greenhouses were shut down, the property put up for sale and prayer ascended for guidance as to the next step. For a year, I worked for a Christian builder on odd building operations, starting at 6.0 a. m. often correcting proofs in the dinner hour, on a rough building site, and then, on reaching home, changing clothes and travelling to London and elsewhere to continue the ministry of the Word.

This was sent by an anonymous reader of the *Berean Expositor* in early days.

THE SERVANT'S PATH IN A DAY OF REJECTION.

Servant of Christ, stand fast amid the scorn
    Of men who little know or love thy Lord;
Turn not aside from toil; cease not to warn,
    Comfort and teach. Trust Him for thy reward;
A few more moment's suffering, and then
    Cometh sweet rest from all thy heart's deep pain.

For grace pray much, for much thou needest grace.
    If men thy work deride, - what can they more?
Christ's weary foot thy path on earth doth trace;
    If thorns wound thee, they piercéd Him before;
Press on, look up, though clouds may gather round;
    Thy place of service He makes hallowed ground.

Have friends forsaken thee, and cast thy name
    Out as a worthless thing? Take courage then;
GO TELL THY MASTER, for they did the same
    To Him, who once in patience toil'd for them;

Yet He was perfect in all service here;
Thou oft has failed; this maketh Him more dear.

Another little sign that the Lord was watching over our movements must now be recorded. The moment our cottage and
nursery were sold, we had to move. Furniture was put in
store, and a temporary home sought. I set out one morning
with three or four addresses of holiday apartments in view,
and called at a bungalow in an adjacent village, named Thun-
dersley. The elderly lady explained the situation, showed the
furnished rooms and facilities but said she was expecting
some one to call that afternoon to conclude an agreement to
take the apartment for the summer. She did ask about children in the event of this agreement falling through. We had
lost a lovely little daughter, named Joy Jeannette as a baby,
and because she died suddenly whilst on a visit to her Grand-
ma's, we had the added ordeal of a coroner's inquest.

By the time we were negotiating the holiday apartment, Ruth,
our third daughter, and the second surviving, was about three
years old. I explained that our children had been brought up
in a home where the Bible was honoured - which I found
pleased the lady well. I felt so convinced that this was to be
our home, that I never inspected the remaining apartments,
and went home and waited. Sure enough a postcard came saying that the summer booking had not been concluded; we paid
a second visit in full strength and the apartment was taken.
Now comes the revealing of the hand of the Lord once again,
another door having closed, another was about to open. The
lady of the bungalow said "would you mind very much if I were
not here to receive you when you arrive?" I replied "If you
do not mind strangers entering in your house, we certainly do
not". She explained that she wished very much to visit a friend
before being tied as it were to the house and away she went.
Upon her return she said "are you Charles H. Welch?" "Do
you know where I have been? I have been visiting the widow of
the late Christopher Smith, Assistant Secretary to Dr. Bullinger". And in the bookcase near where we had sat to have our
first meal, were bound volumes of *"Things to Come" with my own
articles in them!* Out of all the possible places that might
have been provided for our temporary home, this one had been
selected !

Soon after this, the cry from "Macedonia" came in the shape
of a call to Canada, in the interests of a Rightly Divided Word.
This invitation we should not have been free to accept had we
not previously shut down the nursery work and looked for the
next indication. Proverbs 3:5, 6 still worked. The reader
who would like to supplement this notice by a fuller report

should consult Vol. XXXV1, pages 48-53 of the *Berean Exposi-tor* which ends with the following personal testimony of Mr. Fenton. He concluded the meeting thus:

"I just want to say a very brief word. I have enjoyed im-mensely all the meetings we have had. To-night we have had a sample of what we have had practically all through.

"For a man who treats the Scriptures as wonderful and be-lieves every word of it, and who is tolerant with those who may not agree with him on some things, and who is apt to teach, and is thoroughly fundamental in all that the Scriptures teach, believing in it all, I have never met Mr. Welch's equal. There are those who are just as fundamental and just as true to the Word so far as they see it, but Mr. Welch has opened the book to me, and to all of us who have attended the meetings, in a way that has given us a broader and deeper insight into its teaching, so that we cannot dispense with any verse or any word".

When the war broke out in 1949, we were living in our new house at Hutton, and as it became increasingly impossible to plan for meetings ahead with the possibility of air-raids at any time, I undertook the post of Liaison Officer in the Food Office, superintending the recording of all movement either in or out of the neighbourhood, the notifying of the Registrar and the cancellation and transference of rationing permits. This lasted from September 1939 to February 1943, three years and a half (the time of the great tribulation) when out of the blue came a series of letters, showing that a number of friends had simultaneously and without any collusion, felt that in spite of the conditions of the time some move should be made to save the witness from extinction. The result was that Mr Brininger and I met together, and drafted an advertisement which was put into a number of religious journals, asking for news of:

"A Hall, Large Room or any other suitable meeting place, within a few miles of Charing Cross".

but no response was received. We were told that what we sought was an impossibility, as all such rooms and halls were either commandeered or bombed. "Impossible" I said, "yes, but not with the Lord". Sure enough, while I was away in Scot-land, my wife sent on a letter that had been posted in Bath. I opened it and read that the writer had been shown an earlier copy of *The Life of Faith* but expected that after such a lapse of time we were suited. This however was not the case, and Mr. Brininger, Mr. Dive, Mrs. Welch and myself, entered for the first time the Chapel in Wilson Street, E. C. and I looked across the road to the premises that had housed the leather

J

working firm of Jacobs & Sons, where I had been employed some forty years previously.

We learned from the Trustees who met us, that a nephew of Bishop Horsley, some hundred years or more previously, had left the Church of England to be free from a ready made creed, in the desire to follow the teaching of the Scriptures wherever it should lead. We found ourselves meeting with those who were "Berean" in spirit, if not in name. However, an obstacle loomed large in my mind. Here was going to be a temptation of the first magnitude. What would the Trust Deeds impose in the way of the Lord's Supper, for I was determined still to remain homeless rather than yield. Once again the hand of the Lord was revealed. Owing to the strong Roman Catholic influence in the neighbourhood, and to prevent the chapel ever being taken over by that body, the Trust contained this clause, or words to this effect:

> "No one practising Mariolatory or believing in the transubstantiation of the Roman Catholic Mass, can ever hold office in this building".

As the senior Trustee was nearly ninety years of age, I felt it would be somewhat cruel to introduce an argument on the matter of the ordinances but he somehow got hold of a copy of *"The Dispensational Place of the Lord's Supper"* and came back for six copies more! The upshot of this meeting was, that we were granted permission to use the chapel for one year. After this we would meet again and come to a further decision. As the chapel had been closed for years, it took a great deal of labour to put it in a clean enough state for use. Moreover, it had decrepit gas fittings, so bad, that the lighting of one jet, would put another out. At length, the proprietor of a firm in the adjacent building, cut a hole through the wall, and tapped his own electric meter and fitted up two large lamps similar to those used in markets. This was a splendid act of Christian charity which we all appreciated.

We reproduce on the next page, the announcement of the opening Service held on Thursday, September 30th, 1943.

THE OPENING SERVICE

of

THE BIBLE TRAINING CENTRE

on

Thursday, 30th September, 1943, at 5.30 p.m. precisely

ORDER OF SERVICE

RE-OPENING AND RE-DEDICATION

of the

WORK AT WILSON STREET CHAPEL
(The Chapel of the Opened Book)

Chairman:
Mr. Alexander Boyd (Tynemouth)

Hymn 1 ... ..."Sing of the things which Christ hath done".

Prayer.

Reading ... ... Nehemiah 8:1-12. Luke 4:16-21.

Hymn 56 .. ..."God spake in days of old".

Welcome by Mr. H. T. Crewe (Principal Trustee).

Hymn 90 .. ..."Great God of wonders".

Statement by Hon. Secretary, Mr. F. P. Brininger.
Inaugural Address by Mr. Charles H. Welch.

At the close of the Address, the Congregation will stand while the following re-dedication is made in the Name of the Lord:-

RE-DEDICATION

Our gracious God and Father, in the name of Thy Beloved Son, our Saviour Jesus Christ, we thankfully acknowledge the earnest desire for the unsullied Word that led men and women of God in days gone by to search their consciences, to search Thy Word, and eventually to build this House, and for many years to hold fast and to hold forth in this place the "truth as it is in Jesus".

We come into Thy presence on this day of reviving, and humbly re-dedicate this place and all those associated with it to the continued testimony to Thine infallible Scriptures, and to the proclamation of the One Foundation, the One Mediator, and the One Offering of our Lord Jesus Christ, and to the teaching and training of those who shall be raised up in days to come to continue this Witness until that day when all Thy servants, both past, present, and to come, shall stand before Thee and render an account of their stewardship.

With that day in mind we earnestly pray that no sectarian division shall mar our testimony, but that we may ever seek to keep the unity of the Spirit in the bond of peace. Grant, too, our gracious God, that all who now take up this ministry, or shall be associated with it, may stedfastly keep before heart and mind the injunction of the apostle Paul to his son in the faith:

"Study to show thyself approved unto God, a workman that needeth not to be ashamed, rightly dividing the Word of truth". (2 Tim. 2:15).

"Not that we are sufficient of ourselves to think anything as of ourselves but our sufficiency is of God". (2 Cor. 3:5).

Hymn 11 ... ..."Saviour, wher'er Thy people meet".

Prayer and Benediction.

Quite near the Chapel of the Opened Book, are many historic buildings and places.
The Church of St. Giles and Old London Wall.

St Giles. E.C. 2
First built 1090.
Oliver Cromwell married and
John Milton buried here
Piece of old London wall.
CHW/58

Bunhill Fields, where John Bunyan, Dr. John Owen, Daniel
De Foe, and many other Non-conformist worthies are buried,

and the Church of Saint Mary the Virgin, where John Heminge and Henry Condell are remembered for their selfless service in

collecting, preserving and publishing the first folio of the works of Shakespeare.

We must now return for a moment to the house in Hutton, Essex. Apart from an accidental unloading of bombs, we were practically immune from air-raids, although we saw the sky redden in distant London as docks and districts went up in flames. Yet, of what use was the chapel if we lived so far away? It was not a simple matter to decide. I could be blamed for criminal folly, for leaving Hutton, and taking wife and family right into horrible danger. Yet once again, Proverbs 3:5, 6 was indicated. One of my daughters made this remark, for which I could not refrain from expressing my gratitude:

"Dad, there's no need to pray about it. If God has given us the chapel, surely we are not going to ask should we go".

His act necessitated our response. It may be that most readers would not care to let me be responsible for their finances - not because of any suspicion of dishonesty, but because I did such strange things. Yet I have never paid rent for a dwelling in my life. It worked out like this.

When I knew, after twelve years waiting, that it might be possible to be married, I visited a Christian builder living in Ilford, Essex, and inspected some small houses which he was building and which were being sold at £300 freehold. The price seems ridiculous now, but they were well built six room houses with bath room. I learned that the procedure was that a building society would advance £250 and I would put down the rest. I suppose the builder saw the look that passed over my face, for I had still those five dreadful years of little or no income behind me. "If of course the £50 is a difficulty, it could be made a second charge" he said. This was agreed upon, and we immediately reaped the benefit, the house next door paying as rent, just 2/- more per week than we were, who were buying a house. When the break in health drove me into the country, my house was immediately occupied and the builder still collected rent, paid mortgage, cleared gutter, and sent me an account quarterly. After a year had passed he offered to buy the house he had sold me for £300 at the advanced price of £450. I never did want to be a "landlord" so readily agreed. I received a letter however, expressing regret that he had just failed to get his application lodged in time and that the deal would be put off for a month. Had the deal gone through at once I should have lost all, for at that moment Farrow's Bank closed. When the time came to sell our cottage it realized with the nursery I had built £800. The new house built for me at Hutton cost £800, and when we left for London it was sold for £800. I searched London for a suitable house, and saw residences costing two, three or four thousand pounds - all entirely beyond my reach. Eventually Mrs. Welch and I discovered **33**, Union Road, a twelve roomed house, in a much bombed area. It was up for sale freehold for £795. I paid the £95 deposit, and when the time came for the transaction to be completed, the agent said, "before we go further, will you please read this paper". Knowing my lack of business experience, dreading some last minute trap, I could not make head nor tail of the document before us. Seeing my perplexity and understanding what was my difficulty he patiently explained that at his recommendation the Halifax Building Society would advance THE LOT! And I was expecting that with bombs dropping and war raging that they might possibly advance *one third*! The reader will see how it is true that while I have always owned the house in which we live, I have never paid or received a penny - each resale provided for the next move. What a business head! What an all sheltering care!!

Black out conditions made meetings difficult, but they never ceased. Houses went up in dust behind and before, on the right hand and the left, but **33** remained. Seven ceilings had to be taken down and restored. One window at the back of the house was no sooner readjusted than it was blown out into the garden again but we were mercifully spared. Once after a bad night of bombing I went downstairs to discover that the ceiling in my study which housed about 1500 books, had come down, burying my desk with lumps of broken plaster. One piece of paper stood up above the rubbish, and to my surprise I discerned in my own hand writing, the significant words "none of these things move me"! So I waved across to Germany and said "carry on Hitler", and said to the wife, "you have often said, 'Dad your study does want a clean up' - *well its going to need one now!* "

Pages of experiences could be added but we have done what we hoped to do, namely to give a brief account of the choice of and the fashioning of this very earthen vessel, in the hope that some other, in similar adverse circumstances, might be encouraged to "follow the gleam".

We conclude with a sketch of the Pulpit of the Chapel of the Opened Book, and remind readers that we can still supply copies of an original water colour made of the chapel itself by the writer of this record.

The Pulpit
of the
Chapel of the Opened Book

THE BEREAN FORWARD MOVEMENT

OUR ONLY UNITY.—	"The Unity of the Spirit" (Eph. 4:3).
OUR ONE FOUNDATION.—	"Other foundation can no man lay than that is laid, which is Jesus Christ" (1 Cor. 39:11).
OUR ONLY AUTHORITY.—	"All scripture is given by inspiration of God" (2 Tim. 3:16).
OUR GUIDING PRINCIPLE.—	"Rightly dividing the Word of Truth" (2 Tim. 2:15).

The Berean Forward Movement has been formed to *foster* the testimony of Dispensational Truth and to *further* this testimony among young and old.

The London Centre of this movement is

THE CHAPEL OF THE OPENED BOOK

Wilson Street, Finsbury Square, London, E.C.2

Principal: Charles H. Welch

Assistant Principal: Stuart Allen

Hon. Secretary and Treasurer: George T. Foster,

17 Southcote Road, Reading, Berks., England

THE BEREAN PUBLISHING TRUST

The organ of this movement is *The Berean Expositor*, a magazine devoted to the exposition of the Scriptures with special regard to its right division.

At present it is published on alternate months (10d. per copy, 5s. 9d. per annum), to be obtained from the Hon. Distributing Secretary and Treasurer:

LEONARD A. CANNING,

40 Tumblewood Road, Banstead, Surrey, England, from whom all the works indicated on the price list overpage can be obtained.

Price List of Books

Title	s.	d.
Berean Expositor—Annual Subscription ..	5	9
Berean Expositor—Bound Volume (2 years)	12	6
Life Through His Name	15	0
Just and the Justifier	12	6
The Apostle of the Reconciliation	12	6
An Alphabetical Analysis, vols. 1, 2 & 3 each	12	6
,, ,, ,, vol. 8	15	0
From Pentecost to Prison	10	6
Testimony of the Lord's Prisoner	8	6
Parable Miracle and Sign	8	6
Dispensational Truth	12	6
This Prophecy	7	6
The Prize of the High Calling	7	6
The Form of Sound Words	5	0
Ecclesiastes	4	0
The Burden of Prophecy	4	0
Studies in the Book of Job	3	0
Things Most Surely Believed	2	0
Accepted in the Beloved	2	0
Wisdom: Human & Divine	2	0
The Deity of Christ	1	3
Right Division and the Gospel	1	3
Grace and Glory	1	3
The Four Gospels	1	0
True from the Beginning	1	6
United Yet Divided	1	0
Hell	1	0
Far Above All	1	0
Dispensational Place of the Lord's Supper ..		10
The Signs of the Times	1	6
That Blessed Hope		9
Sin and its Relation to God		6
Resurrection (S. Allen)	1	0
The Bride and the Body	2	0
Reconciliation of all Things	2	0
Ephesians via Romans	1	3
Strangers and Sojourners with Me	1	0
The Temple of Truth .. .. per dozen	2	6
Berean Gospel messages .. set of 8		8
Right Division .. .. per dozen	2	0
What is a Christian? .. .. ,, ,,		6
Can We Believe the Bible? .. ,, ,,		6
Berean Pictorial Charts .. set of 13		9
Signpost Magazine—24 articles by A. Harrop	2	0
,, ,, articles by S.Allen ..	2	0
Pentecost (S. Allen)		9
The Church (by S. Allen) .. per dozen	2	0
God's Present Purpose (A. H. Morton) ..	5	6
Berean Hymn Book	2	6
,, ,, ,, Tunes only .. .	8	6

Printed in Great Britain by the Berean Press,
48a London Road, Kingston-on-Thames, Surrey, England.

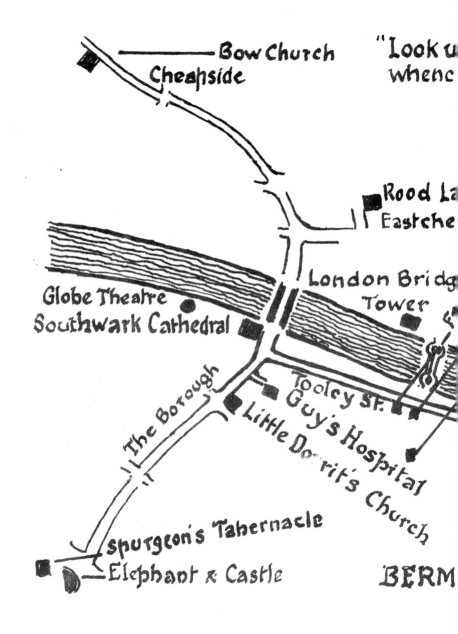

Bow Church
Cheapside

"Look u
whenc

Rood La
Eastche

London Bridg
Tower

Globe Theatre
Southwark Cathedral

The Borough

Tooley St.
Guy's Hospital

Little Dorrit's Church

Spurgeon's Tabernacle
Elephant & Castle

BERM

Truth For Today Bible Fellowship
2508 N. 400E.
Lafayette, IN 47905